Minimalist Living

Decluttering for Joy, Health, and Creativity

By

GENEVIEVE PARKER HILL

For those who seek a simple, joyful life.

Contents

Introduction

Chapter One - Minimalism Is All About You

Chapter Two - For Joy

Chapter Three - For Health

Chapter Four - For Creativity

Chapter Five - Facing Resistance

Chapter Six - Begin Today

Chapter Seven - Creating a Fresh New Space

Chapter Eight - What to Do With All That Stuff

Chapter Nine - Maintaining Minimalism

Chapter Ten - Minimalism and Your Purpose

Resources

Introduction

In the summer of 2004, I was a rising sophomore in college on my first visit to Paris, and I was jubilant. It was midnight; I was riding the metro with a small group of excited international students when the leader of the group I was with handed me her cell phone.

"It's your mother," she said, sounding casual and unworried as only the French can.

I grabbed the phone. "Hi Mom! Guess where I am -- I'm on the Metro in Paris!"

"Baby, are you sitting down?" Her tone instantly got my attention. After all, it was midnight in Paris, and she had called the group leader – a number I didn't even know she had. I sat down. "Our house burned down," she said calmly.

"What?"

"No one was hurt, we're all okay. Even Lando." My heart warmed with relief. My family was okay; even our dog was okay. "But, it was a serious fire. Most of the house is damaged."

That fire was the beginning of my transformation from a dedicated pack rat to a joyful minimalist. Today, my family counts the fire as one of the major blessings to occur in our lives. It showed us the love of our community, and it taught us that value lies in relationships, not in things.

Of course, losing almost everything was bittersweet. I still feel sad over the loss of a shelf full of my childhood and teenage journals, some loving and meaningful letters written to me, the doll cradle my grandpa made for me, and some toys I had treasured and hoped to give to my future children. But even as I feel the loss, I wonder where I would put those mementos now. I don't have room in my budget for a storage space, and I'm currently living the life of an international vagabond – and loving how easy it is to travel and move without too much baggage.

The loss of my sentimental things in the fire, and the ensuing years of frequent travel and moves, taught me that value doesn't live in things – *it lives in our relationship to those things and our relationships with each other*. Relationships are intangible -- bonds built in our hearts and minds, and that is good news. It means we don't have to hold on to possessions. Rather, we can find ways to value each other, our stories, our memories, and our histories that don't involve renting mini-storage units or having walk- in closets in every room.

I wrote this book because I sense a longing within so many for more. More joy, more space, more time. I want to share what I was lucky enough to accidentally discover - that a life that values relationships and experiences over ownership and consumerism can be freer and more fulfilling. But how and why is it more fulfilling? And how do we create this life when the idea of decluttering even one room or space can be overwhelming and exhausting to think about?

I wrote this book to help answer those questions. I surveyed dozens of people and conducted interviews for *Minimalist Living*. In addition, I've held dialogues on the Facebook page at www.facebook.com/mnmlstlvng (which you are invited to follow). It's my hope that the collective wisdom of the people I've talked to about minimalist living, along with what I've gleaned from my research and my post-fire attitude shift, will inspire you and give you practical ways to live a more joyful, minimalist life.

I want to warn you. Simply reading this book won't do anything. You've got to take action. But I promise we will make it fun. It'll be fun in a challenging way. It's my job to break down the many steps toward becoming a person who doesn't live with clutter so that you don't feel overwhelmed. You can simply follow the steps and discover that you have become a joyful minimalist.

First, we'll talk about the definitions of minimalism, and what it means for the purposes of this book. Then, we'll address the major ways minimalist living can bring you more joy, better health, and abundant creativity. Those first four chapters will also give you some practical advice when it comes to making more time in your schedule and creating a more peaceful inner life. Once we're inspired, we'll get practical and jump into facing the resistance that can block your path to minimalist living. Next, we'll get started, with techniques, tips, and strategies for turning your home and your time into a healthy, creative haven and keeping it that way. Finally, we'll talk about the deeper reasons to be a minimalist including what it has to do with your inner life and your greater purpose here.

I'm so excited to take this journey with you. Let's get started.

CHAPTER ONE

Minimalism Is All About You

"We no longer live in a material world. Sorry Madonna." – Natalie Sisson

Let's start by talking about the word behind the phrase "minimalist living."

Minimalism.

The word "minimalism" comes to us from the world of art and design. It's the less-is-more aesthetic that you've experienced if you've ever been in an art museum and found yourself pondering a canvas simply painted in one solid color.

I use minimalism here to describe a similar attitude toward our belongings, our thoughts, and our lives. When I talk about minimalism, I mean something that is different for each person. Although minimalism in this context isn't the term used to describe a certain style of art or design, some of the connotations from that world can inform our definitions of minimalism. For example, to some, minimalism means clean lines, white space, simplicity, and a less-is-more mentality. But that conventional definition of minimalism won't necessarily apply to everyone as they think about what kind of place they want their home to be or what they want their life to look like.

Within this context, what do we mean exactly when we say "I'm a minimalist?" Well, the answer varies for each person, but first and foremost, a minimalist lifestyle is about increasing your joy through simplicity. It's all about what makes *you* happy, and nothing more.

What Minimalism Is and Isn't

Minimalism is:

- Letting go of that which does not serve you.

- Designing your life based on how you want to live it, not the expectations of others.

- Letting go of negative or obsessive thoughts.

- Looking around and seeing your personality reflected in your living space.

- Being surrounded by colors and textures that make you feel good.

- Putting furniture in rooms to reflect how you really live, instead of how other people live.

- Creatively using one item for more than one purpose.

- Borrowing from friends or neighbors, or renting, if you use something rarely.

- Giving unused things away now, not later.

- Knowing that you have what you need and it is enough.

- Spending money on experiences and adventures.

Minimalism is not:

- Saying "yes" to every request of your time.

- Keeping things out of guilt or a sense of loyalty to someone.

- Making sure your home looks like it could be in a décor magazine (unless that's truly your passion).

- Having a couch and a TV just because everyone else does.

- Having a gadget for every possible whim you might have.

- Filling an attic, garage, or basement with things for the kids in case they ever want them.

- Keeping something because it's easier than recycling it or giving it away.

- Keeping something only because it's worth a lot of money.

- Renting a personal storage unit.

- Spending money on possessions that require maintenance or management.

A Consumer Culture

In the U.S. and many developed nations, we live in a culture that is defined by consuming. It doesn't have to be that way for individuals, but it takes tremendous effort not to be influenced by the culture, and most of us are influenced in ways that we don't even realize. Being influenced by our culture is normal and acceptable – except in cases where a cultural attitude is damaging. Consumerism is one of those attitudes that can be very damaging.

Consuming in itself is normal, something that all humans have done since the beginning of time. We consume food and we create tools and art for our use and enjoyment. These things don't last forever, so we create more. In that way, we've always been consumers and we always will be consumers. However, the concept of a consumer culture is one that every person aiming to enjoy a simpler and richer lifestyle must question.

In the 1930s and '40s, the Great Depression and World War II made a consumer-based lifestyle much more difficult and less common than it is today. Belongings were handmade, or if store-bought, were carefully maintained and repaired so that they could be of use for years. These careful measures were both a necessity as well as a patriotic duty during wartime. After World War II, we entered what Lizabeth Cohen in her book *A Consumers' Republic: The Politics of Mass Consumption in Postwar America* calls "an economy, culture, and politics built around the promises of mass consumption." She argues that the current consumer culture in the U.S., and the idea that consuming could be a patriotic duty, is a product of the complex political soup of postwar America and had deep and far-reaching consequences. The consuming part of the American Dream – the buying of more and more part – continues today, aided by the advertising industry.

One beloved American pastime, watching television, has historically been a conduit for fueling our desire to consume. Today, advertising is moving to the internet, but television advertising remains an important shaper of the collective American – and global – consciousness.

The television industry developed over time as a platform to sell advertising space. TV broadcasts are selected and scheduled by how many viewers will tune in to watch each show. Advertisers pay millions of dollars to have their messages seen and heard alongside popular broadcasts. The reason that companies are willing to invest so much in television advertisements is that these commercials are extremely influential. They begin influencing us almost from birth. When my sister and I were little girls, around five and seven years old, we started seeing TV commercials for a doll called California Roller Baby. We begged my mom for the doll, but she said no, instantly sensing that Roller Baby was not a high-quality product. But the ads were so colorful, and Roller Baby really skated. She had little knee pads, a skimpy helmet that showed most of her platinum blond hair, an early '90s Santa Monica skater outfit, and the body and face of a toddler. Her life was a carefree and perfect blend of childhood fun and adult freedom. We begged. Mom still didn't want to buy the dolls, but when my grandmother heard about our wishes, she bought us each a California Roller Baby for Christmas. We were thrilled when we opened them, and then disappointed. Roller Baby was smaller than she'd seemed on TV, and her skating ability was jerky and mechanical. She began falling apart within weeks. Mom said that our grandmother had given us the Roller Baby dolls to teach us a lesson about TV advertising. It worked.

What is the message of most ads? The typical message is not, "Buy this product," but rather, "Someone like you – maybe someone slightly happier, hipper, and thinner – enjoys this product. In fact, it makes his or her whole life perfect." The message is about your identity, and what it requires for you to think of yourself in a certain way. The mind games and manipulations of advertisers are often so clever that we are largely unaware of the ways that they affect us. Fifteen years after seeing the commercial for California Roller Baby, I moved to Santa Monica and jogged alongside the California skating babes on the famous beach-side pave way, although I could never bring myself to buy skates. Who knows, but maybe my move to Santa Monica was partly because somewhere in my brain, something had been telling me for fifteen years that the California roller babies had the good life.

As a less far-fetched example of how far advertisers' manipulations of our concepts of identity go, think about clothing. We can purchase clothes that have brands emblazoned on them. It's free advertising for the brands – advertising that we pay for by purchasing the clothes and becoming walking billboards. This phenomenon proves that people aren't only buying things for the quality or usefulness, or even the beauty of the clothes, but because they want to be associated with a certain sensibility, an adventurous spirit, elegance, or sex-appeal, for example. Whatever brand they choose fits into the self-identity they desire. Brands work very hard and spend millions to cultivate these associations through advertising.

Marketing companies go so far as to invent needs that the average person perhaps doesn't even know he or she has. This is not limited to the U.S. In India, marketing messages for a feminine wash (which many gynecologists recommend women avoid) tell women they can be "fairer" by using the wash on their intimate areas.[1] It

1   Sarah C. Nelson, "Vagina 'Brightener': Indian Feminine Hygiene Product Promises To Make Genitals 'Many Shades Fairer'" The Huffington Post United Kingdom, April 12, 2012, http://www.huffingtonpost.co.uk/2012/04/12/vagina-brightener-indian-feminine-hygiene-product-promises-to-make-genitals-many-shades-fairer_n_1420052.html.

strikes me that many women may never consider that they want to change the color of their private parts, much less need to do so in the face of the health risks that come from using feminine washes, until they see advertisements like these.

Advertisements in any medium are illusions. Sometimes they are beautiful, artistically-created illusions that we can enjoy just like we enjoy seeing a good movie. But our subconscious may not be able to recognize that they are illusions. Even though we know that there was a director, set designer, actors, maybe even a composer, and various artists involved in making a TV commercial, the messages can still get in. And we may get a prompt from our subconscious when we are out shopping to buy a certain brand, or even to buy a product that we didn't know we wanted before we saw the ad

We are also primed to purchase simply by the experience of shopping in super stores. This may not be something we always notice, but it has an effect on us. My husband and I moved to a 3rd world country where shops are small and poorly stocked. We eventually got used to shopping in many different stores, and not always being able to purchase exactly what we wanted. Then we returned to the US. The experience of walking the aisles of a US grocery store after living abroad is overwhelming. It feels like on onslaught, and the heightened experience makes me buy either too much, or simply want to give up and leave the store. This tells me that we are psychologically affected by our superstores and that affects our buying habits.

Rest assured, we are the captains of our own ships. It simply takes focused effort and intentional living to defy the consumer culture in which we live and to pursue life as we truly desire on a deep soul level. Resistance of the consumer-based lifestyle that is the norm in the U.S. began to take hold of the popular imagination in the '60s, as people rejected consumerism and a host of other conventional ways of thinking. Living a more minimal life has been in vogue on and off over the years and has been called "downsizing," "simple living," "de-cluttering," and, more recently, "minimalism."

We can build fulfilling, meaningful, joyful lives without filling our homes with junk. What is more, we can bless other people with cast-offs while still remembering the important place those belongings had for us. We can also use the newfound space in our lives to have more joy, better health, more creativity, and to fulfill our purpose. The way to do this is to embrace minimalism – as you define it.

The Life You Want

Throughout your reading of this book, and as you go about simplifying your life for more joy, don't hold to anyone's definition of minimalism but your own. For one person, minimalism is selling off a second home or investment properties that take time and money to manage. For another, a minimalist life could mean selling a home and living in an RV while traveling the country.

Your task as you read this book and simplify your life is to identify what purpose each item, thought, and commitment serves for you. You can design your life, manage your own time, and create your ideal living environment.

Design it Now

Let's think about what we want now in our homes, our days, and our inner lives. Spend five minutes journaling or sketching what you want your home to look and feel like.

It could be a clean, spare space that will best show off your collection of modern art. It could be a serene escape full of meditation cushions and hammocks perfect for afternoon naps by the sea. It could be a cozy apartment with everything in its place and nothing extra. It could be a home with a photography backdrop instead of a formal dining room. You are limited only by your imagination. Define what you need your home to be for you, and then stick to it. Don't feel guilty about how you choose to design your space.

Now spend five minutes writing about what you want your days to look like. How do you want to spend your time? Do you want to change jobs so that you can work less or enjoy your work more? Would you like to spend more time with loved ones, more time painting, or more time building camp stoves from recycled cans? Don't think about limitations such as debt, bills, or other's expectations right now. Simply dream about all the ways you'd like to spend your time in an ideal world. This will be your guide as you simplify your schedule for more joy.

Finally, take five more minutes to journal about your inner life. Would you like to be happier? Have less self-doubt? Be more positive? Laugh more? Be more open to love, spontaneity, or adventure? Write about the ways your inner life could use a makeover. Write about the ways that your thoughts might be out of control. After all, everything starts with a thought. How can your thoughts serve you better? Having control over the thoughts you let into your mind is just like having control over the items you let into your home or the commitments you let into your schedule: it takes practice, but it is possible.

Why Now?

So why have you decided to read this book now? Why are you investigating the possibility of simplifying your life? Many people begin to think about changing their surroundings before, during, or after a big life transition.

You may be moving. You could be downsizing to a smaller home or apartment and you know all your material possessions won't fit in the new place. Or maybe you're moving into a bigger abode, but you simply don't want to move all of your stuff because you know you don't need or want all of it (not to mention concerns about the money and muscle required to move it). Perhaps you just finished moving and you don't want to go through the insanity of moving all your knick knacks ever again.

Other big transitions can motivate us to simplify as well. Starting a new job can make us want to simplify everything else. Getting married or moving in together can encourage us to seek a fresh start in our relationship to each other and to our things. Perhaps you're an empty-nester for the first time, and you need to make your home and your life reflect your life as it is today, not as it was with kids in the house.

Perhaps you just find yourself feeling inspired to make a change. Maybe it's New Years and you've got some resolutions to keep. Maybe it's a new moon. You can have any reason you want to be here. Now that you're here, how far do you want to go?

All Kinds of Minimalists

Minimalists fall on a spectrum. Where you fall on this spectrum is based on your personality and expressed in how many belongings you will end up with when your simplifying project is finished. Some minimalists, having tasted the freedom of lightening their load, become obsessed with how few belongings they can own and still thrive. They may choose a number, say 100, and live with no more than 100 belongings. Or, like ultra-minimalist vagabond Andrew Hyde, who lived for a time with only 15 things, they really push the limits. If this fascinates you, go for it.

More likely, you'll find yourself comfortable being a more moderate kind of minimalist. These folks don't count how many things they own, nor do they particularly care. What's important to them is that they are not overwhelmed or stressed by their stuff. They want to have what they find enjoyable and useful on hand and nothing more. In fact, you could say that most people probably *want* to fit in this category, but they don't know how to get there. Few people like the heavy feeling that comes from knowing there are hundreds of boxes with contents unknown stashed away in various places.

Now that you've identified why you'd like to declutter, where you feel comfortable on the range of minimalism, and how it's possible to define minimalism for yourself, it's time to get inspired by the tremendous benefits that paring down can bring to your home, your schedule, and your happiness level.

CHAPTER TWO

For Joy

"Not what we have but what we enjoy, constitutes our abundance."
— Epicurus

Before I became a minimalist, whenever I would do a major cleaning of my house, I'd discover projects and items that I loved the idea of completing, but that I forgot about and never got around to.

Back in late 2011, I gave away and sold a lot of things because I want to only have the projects around that I am truly passionate about - things that bring me joy. This way I won't forget the important things. It won't be: "out of sight, out of mind." What is it that you want to be "in sight and in mind" these days? Are there hidden treasures in your environment? Would you like to become a minimalist, thereby becoming a healthier, more creative and joyful individual?

If so, you must choose. More than motivation, more than inspiration, more than a wish or a dream, you need to make a decision. Reading a book about minimalism is a good step in the right direction, but your life will only change if you take action. Decide now to act. We must decide that a new identity as a minimalist will replace our old identification with our belongings and activities. To choose to change, we need a compelling reason. And what greater reason is there than a deep sense of contentment?

To discover why minimalist living can bring us an abundance of joy, let's take a closer look at happiness.

The Science of Joy

A 2006 BBC News article by Mike Rudin addressed findings in the field of positive psychology — the study of what makes people happy. Studies show that the top three things that bring lasting joy are relationships, meaning, and goals. The article states:

"First, family and friends are crucial - the wider and deeper the relationships with those around you the better. It is even suggested that friendship can ward off germs. Our brains control many of the mechanisms in our bodies which are responsible for disease. Just as stress can trigger ill health, it is thought that friendship and happiness can have a protective effect."[2]

On meaning and goals, the article had this to say about the results of happiness studies:

---

2   Professor Ed Diener, quoted in Mike Rudin, "The Science of Happiness," *BBC News*, April 30, 2006,http://news.bbc.co.uk/2/hi/programmes/happiness_formula/4783836.stm.

"The second vital ingredient is having meaning in life, a belief in something bigger than yourself - from religion, spirituality or a philosophy of life. The third element is having goals embedded in your long term values that you're working for, but also that you find enjoyable."[3]

Psychologists argue that we need to find fulfillment through having goals that are interesting to work on and which use our strengths and abilities.

So deep friendship, a sense of meaning, and value-based goals are all ingredients in the soup of happiness. What has never been scientifically proven is that more possessions bring more joy. In fact, happiness researcher Daniel Kahneman of Princeton University said, "Standard of living has increased dramatically and happiness has increased not at all, and in some cases has diminished slightly."[4]

Journalist and founder of eco-blog *TreeHugger.com* Graham Hill found his own happiness diminishing after he very quickly earned a fortune from the sale of his internet startup in the late '90s. Post-sale, he spent time and energy buying a large home and outfitting it with all the fancy gadgetry money could buy. He even bought his dream car and hired a personal shopper, but says that "Somehow this stuff

---

3   Ibid.

4   Professor Daniel Kahneman, quoted in Mike Rudin, "The Science of Happiness," *BBC News*, April 30, 2006.http://news.bbc.co.uk/2/hi/programmes/happiness_formula/4783836.stm.

ended up running my life, or a lot of it; the things I consumed ended up consuming me. My circumstances are unusual (not everyone gets an Internet windfall before turning 30), but my relationship with material things isn't."[5] Hill's happiness levels increased when he jettisoned all the extra gadgets and focused on the basics: a fulfilling romance; meaningful pursuits like travel; and his passion, entrepreneurship.

In a 2013 study, the Northwestern University psychologist Galen V. Bodenhausen connected acquisitional attitudes with negative emotions and actions. His results suggested that "irrespective of personality, in situations that activate a consumer mind-set, people show the same sorts of problematic patterns in well-being, including negative affect and social disengagement."[6]

Stuff = Stress

Let's think about the typical process we go through when we acquire something – when we begin our relationship to a belonging. We'll call this example thing a gadget. Think of this process of

---

5   Graham Hill, "Living With Less. A Lot Less." *New York Times,* March 9, 2013, www.nytimes.com.

6   Galen V. Bodenhausen, "Consumerism and its antisocial effects can be turned on—or off," *Association for Psychological Science,* April 9, 2012, http://www.psychologicalscience.org/index.php/news/releases/consumerism-and-its-antisocial-effects-can-be-turned-onor-off.html

acquiring something as applying not just to new gadgets, but also to things we let into our schedules - new commitments and new projects.

First, we buy or are given the gadget. It's such a wonderful new addition to our lives. We've always wanted one, and now we have the newest, coolest, most high-quality gadget on the market. It's going to make our lives easier and more fun. We will be happy, attractive, successful, healthy, and rich because we own this gadget.

We take our gadget home, and now we need to take it out of its packaging. The first ping of stress happens, because it's packaged in hard plastic, and we have to wrestle with it and pinch our fingers getting it open.

Then we throw the packaging away, and feel some more stress about the environment and that giant floating trash island the size of Texas that is out in the Pacific somewhere.

We use and enjoy our gadget for a time, but then it breaks. So then we hire a professional or take it to a shop for repair. It turns out our gadget just needed cleaning and maintenance. This maintenance time takes away from our loved ones and our larger life goals, adding stress as we ask ourselves *where does the time go?*

Life is busy and it's not always easy to remember to clean our gadget when so many other things call for our attention: our jobs, relationships, and other activities. With everything going on, the gadget just sits there, gathering dust. One day we are decluttering the living room, and we see the dusty old gadget. It's taking up much-needed space, and we need to find a different place to store it. Somewhere out of the way.

Briefly a thought occurs to us: *Will I use this again? Maybe I should give it away. Well, I'll probably use it sometime in the future. Just not right now. Anyway, I'm cleaning up. I don't have time to deal with dusting this off and finding a new home for it. Maybe I'll use it later.*

With that, we put it on a high shelf in a closet or in a box in the attic, straining our neck and back in the process.

Then, much later, we think that it would be nice to use the gadget. We look for it, but we can't find it amongst the overwhelming amount of stuff in the closet or attic. After getting dirty and dusty, we promise ourselves we will clean out our home, but for some reason, we put it off.

This stressful process is how our homes become stuffed full of things we don't need. And our homes are certainly packed full in the U.S., an idea brought home in the book *Material World: Global Family Portrait*, by Peter Menzel, Charles C. Mann, and Paul Kennedy. The book contains photographs of statistically average families from around the world, shown with all their belongings in front of their homes. Check out the book and compare the piles of belongings from homes in the U.S compared with the rest of the world. According to Annie Leonard of the *Story of Stuff Project*, in the U.S. we are using more than our share of resources to make our products and support our lifestyle. Although the U.S. comprises only 5% of the world's population, we are using 30% of the world's resources and making 30% of the world's waste. Globally, in the past thirty years, one third of the planet's natural resource space has been consumed. There are many, many environmental reasons to decrease the amount of material goods we consume, including the heartbreaking fact that 80% of the Earth's original forests are gone.[7] And the stress that our over-consuming habits place on us as individuals and on our planet is just one of many compelling reasons to simplify.

Life is Short – Enjoy Your Stuff

Stuff is not evil. We enjoy what we own– when we use it. In fact, our belongings can bring great joy to our lives when they help us connect to each other or pursue meaning and goals. But there's only time for so many pastimes. There are only twenty-four hours in the day. We may dream of the dinner parties we'll throw, the golf we'll play, or the songs we'll write, but if we aim to do too much, we may simply spend our time moving, sorting, and maintaining our

---

7   Karen de Seve, "Welcome to My Jungle... Before It's Gone (Rainforests)," http://www.thefreelibrary.com/Welcome+to+my+jungle+...+before+it's+gone.+(R ainforests).-a084307435

paraphernalia rather than enjoying it. It's unlikely that when we find ourselves bored, the existence of the gadget in the attic is going to occur to us and we are going to dig it out, dust it off, put in fresh batteries and enjoy it.

The purpose of minimalist living is to get us to a point where every single thing we have in our homes is something that brings us ongoing joy or provides usefulness regularly. The journey to a minimalist life can be exhausting and long, but the purpose of this book is to make it easier and more fun. We can make the process itself joyful if we make a strong decision, and keep in mind our "why," our biggest reason for minimalist living.

Giving for Joy

Another truth is that as you simplify, you'll probably end up giving away belongings to friends or charity. The act of giving leads to joy. Kelly Palace, my aunt, had an entire wardrobe of cold weather clothes, formal, professional attire, as well as casual wear. After moving to Florida, Aunt Kelly didn't need most of her clothes – she was able to dress more casually and for the warmer climate. So what she did was spread her entire old wardrobe out on the floor, take a picture of it, and post the photo to Facebook with a short message that said, "This is an entire wardrobe for a woman who is a size 4-6, and it's free to anyone who will come take it off my hands."

What happened was wonderful. A woman came and picked it up. She gave it to a friend who had just escaped an abusive relationship and had left most of her clothes in her old home. This act of giving was a blessing for the woman who received the clothes, but also for Aunt Kelly, who told the story with so much joy. It gave her a lot of pleasure to be able to give the things she didn't need to someone who really needed them.

When Florida artist Cheri Cruden's company downsized and she lost her job, she decided to move across the state so she could be with the man who is now her husband. When they moved in together, they had her furniture, his furniture, and furniture from his parents and his ex-wife all crowded together in one home. In addition, the closets were filled with ghosts from his less-than-happy past, including his ex-wife's wedding dress, despite the fact that they had divorced fifteen years ago. Although it was difficult, the two drastically downsized their belongings. Cheri, a cancer survivor, had learned, as she says, "the importance of trying to possess only what you need."

While they were overseeing the ensuing giant garage sale, something beautiful happened. I'll let you read about it in Cheri's own words:

All the neighbors came by and I was selling lots of stuff. Then this lady and her husband came by. I instantly was attracted to her humor and warmth. She stayed quite a while, and during that time we talked about many things. [...]We talked about her shop in Cocoa and she gave me her card and I promised to stop in some time. During the course of this conversation I learned about the homeless people that came into her shop hoping for a coat, or some pans, or something to make their lives a little easier on the street. Well, I looked around and I had lots of very nice clothes hanging there. I wasn't going back to the corporate world so I would not need them. I had shoes, clothing, blankets, etc., all of which would help someone else. So I offered anything and everything she could fit in her truck.

[...] It was a very rewarding and uplifting experience. To rid oneself of miscellaneous stuff feels very good. You feel light and clean and good.

For Cheri, giving away a truckload of belongings was an incredible way to start a beautiful new relationship, one that makes her feel like "the luckiest woman alive." Decluttering not only provided her love life with a fresh start, it also enabled her to improve the lives of those less fortunate. This gave her a sense of joy and fulfillment.

Designing a Joyful Life

Minimalist living applies not just to your belongings, but to your time. Do you find yourself feeling like you spend your days putting out metaphorical fires and responding to crises from every corner? Do you feel out of control of your days and wonder where the hours go? If so, you may want to declutter your schedule. Take control of your time so that you can spend your days enjoying relationships, connecting to your spirit, and pursuing purposeful goals. If you aren't sure where the time goes, you may want to use a computer tool like Toggl to track your time for a week and see how you spent it. Being an anchorless boat tossed about by the oceans of TV-watching, web-surfing, over-commitment, or other people's expectations can mar your joy just as much as overstuffed closets.

How do we let go of the extra activities in our schedule so that we can enjoy freedom of time? It's not always easy. If you've committed to something, backing out can feel like a blow to your integrity. Yet your own joy is most important, because your happiness spreads. If you're doing something with stress or resentment, you may as well not be doing it. You aren't doing anyone any favors by doing something with a negative attitude.

The home or work environment you create with your belongings can also directly affect how you spend your time. For example, have you ever wished you could watch less TV and paint or (insert activity of choice here) more? Where is your television? Does it have pride of place as the focal point of your living room? What if, instead of your television, that was the spot where your easel and painting supplies were?

I ask these questions to illustrate what a strong impact our home environment has on us. The average American watches almost three hours of television per day.[8] For someone born now who will live to age eighty, that's a total of eight years of television watching – straight, not including time for sleeping. Said another way, TV-watching for the average American is like having a full-time, 40-hour-per-week job for over more than thirty years. If someone replaced this television time with growth activities, say, attending medical school or learning to compose music, he or she could become an expert in seven different fields according to Dr. K. Anders Ericsson's theory of 10,000 hours.[9]

I'd argue that our excessive television watching is at least partly due to the fact that it's so common to own a TV; it's odd *not* to have one. As humans, we are very good at responding and interacting with our environment. Evolutionarily, to survive and thrive in cave-

---

8   US Department of Labor, Bureau of Labor Statistics, *American Time Use Survey Summary,* June 30, 2013, http://www.bls.gov/news.release/atus.nro.htm.

9   Popularized in the book *Outliers: The Story of Success* by Malcolm Gladwell.

person world, we needed to investigate, understand, play with, cultivate, and interact with our surroundings. Humans live all over the globe in all kinds of climates. We are excellent adapters. What is around us is what we will place our attention on. We can use this understanding of the way our brain naturally works to help us do the things that we've always wanted to do, or know we should do for increased vitality, contribution, and joy, but that aren't habits for us yet. If we don't use this knowledge, we may fall victim to our surroundings, such as the TV in our living room that steals so many years of life from the average American.

Using this knowledge about the way we are wired to adapt to our environment looks like this: if you want to eat healthily, get rid of the junk food and replace it with wholesome food. If you want to improve your sleep, remove everything from your bedroom except your comfortable, well-clothed bed. If you'd like to be more sociable, remove your computer and books, and replace them with a big dinner table, games, and comfortable, welcoming décor. If you'd like to be more introspective, remove your big dinner table and games, and install an armchair and a nice lamp surrounded by books, notebooks, pens, and highlighters.

You see where I'm going with this. Options are overrated; they tend to overwhelm us and lead to mediocre lives. When we have too many options, we spend our lives maintaining those options instead of exercising them. In the worlds of cinema and writing, forced economies often lead to creative brilliance. Directors who are forced to work with a limited budget create better films than those given carte blanche, who often create only sound and fury that won't be remembered long past opening night. Poets given a form - meter and rhyming sequence - to work within, find ingenious new images and ways to use words that they perhaps otherwise wouldn't have. In the same way, giving yourself limits in your household, limits on how much you will have and what sort of things you will have, can create more brilliance in your life.

"But I like having options," you may be thinking. "After all, I like to read, and I like to socialize. Can't I do both?" Of course you can, and you should. You should have variety in your life.

However, right now in your life, what do you intuitively know is going to be good for your overall joy? You can always change things later, and you can always go out of your home for variety. In fact, you should. Get out and experience the world. Home needn't be a place that meets all of your needs and desires for entertainment, connection, and every possible hobby that you've ever enjoyed. Create your home so its environment feeds into the essential values and goals of your life -- only the essentials.

Timothy Ferris, productivity expert and celebrity author of *The Four-Hour Workweek*, engages in what he terms a "low-information diet." This allows him to do with his time what we are attempting to with our homes: clear out the non-essentials to make room for life as we desire it. In the same way that I'm advising you to rearrange and de-stuff your home, Ferris' advice is unconventional. He opens his chapter on this concept with: "Cover the baby's ears. I'm going to tell you something that upsets a lot of people." He then goes on to explain that he never watches the news and hardly ever reads the paper. He continues, naming more information that he chooses to ignore.

I realize that cultivating a "low-stuff diet," to modify his phrase, is unconventional and potentially shocking to some. However, if you've come this far, chances are you're open to it and are beginning to see that this new way of life, although initially challenging, will bring new opportunities for growth, fun, and connection. Be inspired by the core message of Chris Guillebeau, author and blogger at The Art of Non-Conformity. He writes, "You don't have to live your life the way other people expect you to." His message shines out of every page he writes, and that one simple idea has inspired people all over the world. Let it free you.

Letting Go of That Which Does Not Serve You

Try as I might, I can't find the author of this quote I first heard in a yoga class: "Let go of that which does not serve you." As we close this chapter on minimalist living for joy, let's address how this idea of letting go applies not only to our things and our activities, but to our thoughts. Gretchin Rubin, author of *The Happiness Project*, writes "You're not happy unless you think you're happy." And I would add that you can think yourself happy. Just like learning to control what you let into your home and your schedule can increase your joy, so can learning to control what thoughts you allow to spend time in your mental landscape. I say "spend time," because it's not always necessary or possible to control impulsive thoughts. Having random negative thoughts flit in and out of the brain is normal. What we want to focus on controlling is how long we spend dwelling on thoughts that make us unhappy.

The best strategy for minimizing the hang out time of negative thoughts isn't to forcefully banish them (which never works) but rather, to replace them with thoughts that make you happy. Everything starts with a thought, so keep your mental garden well-weeded. That's a lot easier when most of the soil is taken up by strong blooming flowers. One caveat: don't allow guilt over negative thinking to be yet another negative thought. If you find yourself suddenly conscious that you're feeling unhappy, examine your thoughts, and then be grateful for them. They provided you with an opportunity to make a change and grow. Every conscious moment is a chance to choose joy. See if you can turn the thoughts around. There is always a silver lining, even if it's small and in need of dusting.

I hope this chapter has given you some strong reasons to simplify your life for more joy. My wish for you is that minimizing what you have maximizes your joy. Next, let's look at how minimalist living can maximize your health in many different ways.

CHAPTER THREE

For Health

"If you haven't got your health, then you haven't got anything." — Count Rugen in *The Princess Bride*

When it was time for a change in Australian minimalist Betty Tolhurst's life, she decided to renovate her home. She replaced her tiles and carpeting with bamboo flooring. This new floor meant that it was easier to keep her home clean. Bamboo is a more renewable surface material than other kinds of wood, so her actions were also healthier for the planet. On top of that, her cleaner home may contribute to increased physical health for Tolhurst, and even more brain power.

Health is a compelling reason to start living a minimalist lifestyle. Tolhurst's renovation is a great example of minimalist living for a healthier life and planet. Many minimalists report that one of their favorite benefits of decluttering is a greater ease in cleaning their homes. Without all the knick-knacks and unneeded stuff, cleaning up takes less time. And with a schedule that leaves you with free time, cleaning can actually happen without stress or undue hurry. If, like Betty, you design your home for your own well-being and that of the planet, you may find yourself replacing hard-to-clean fixtures or even moving into a smaller, more manageable home. As always when embracing minimalism, let go of other people's expectations when creating your life. It's a lot easier to move into a smaller home if you can let go of the idea of a big home as a trophy, or sign of your achievement. If you're working hard so that one day you can own a large home, you may want to rethink that plan. After all, if you aren't enjoying your life and work now, chances are that's not going to change later.

Physical Health

If making space in your life means having more time to clean, you're doing your body all sorts of favors. First of all, the decluttering process in itself is great exercise. We sort, dust, vacuum, and lift. As long as we don't strain any muscles or injure ourselves in the process of cleaning, the exercise is good for us. Just make sure that, if you're inspired to clean during your decluttering process, you use environmentally friendly cleaning products that don't have dangerous chemicals in them or high levels of VOCs (volatile organic compounds). You can find an independently reviewed list of cleaning products graded according to the danger to human health and the environment at *EWG.org/guides/cleaners*.

So you have the actual physical workout of moving and cleaning during the decluttering process, but beyond that, by getting rid of a lot of our things, the health risks associated with uncleanliness decrease. The more we own, the less likely it is that we'll have time and energy to clean it all or the money to have it professionally cleaned. When we don't clean enough, our homes can have increased levels of viruses, bacteria, particulates, endotoxins, molds, and allergens. Our indoor environment can make us sick or listless. In a study of an elementary school in Washington, D.C, when the school was thoroughly cleaned with modern techniques and equipment as well as renovated, students showed increased passing math scores on standardized tests increased by 51%. Attendance increased by 4.5 percent.[10] These improvements came with no changes to teachers, curriculum, or technologies. These results suggest that living in a clean environment can effectively make you smarter. We can certainly conclude that cleaning and renewing our homes can have a significant positive impact on our health.

Another physical health benefit that can come from the minimizing process is that you can make room for new, healthy habits. For example, when Dr. Christiane Northrup began taking tango lessons, she freed herself of her formal dining room set, which she rarely used anyway. Her dining room became her dance hall. She

---

10   Stephen P. Ashkin, "The all-purpose solution," *American School & University*, October 1, 2003, http://ashkingroup.com/pdfs/Education/ashkin%20asu%20october%202003.pdf
.

used the newly open space to practice her new dance skills, allowing it to become not just a form of exercise but a passion that brought new friends and admirers to her life. She could invite friends to dance with her in her new ballroom, all because she was willing to let go of the furniture. She could have said to herself, "Oh, I have this new hobby, the tango, and I like it, but there's really no room in my home, so I'm not going to be able to practice much." Instead, she took action. She released whatever emotional or sentimental investment she had in the furniture. She acknowledged that she rarely had formal dining needs, and then she allowed her stuff to fill a need in someone else's life.

If making space in your life leads to a new romance, the rekindling of an old flame, or even more time to stoke the fires of an already great marriage, you could get an additional benefit from simplifying. Psychological scientist Barbara L. Fredrickson studies emotions from a biological perspective including what the feeling of love — which she calls "positivity resonance" — does to the human body. According to Fredrickson, "The love you do or do not experience today may quite literally change key aspects of your cellular architecture next season and next year - cells that affect your physical health, your vitality, and your overall wellbeing." Most people desire love in their lives, but the scientific research showing that love boosts our immune systems and lengthens our lives might just be the extra motivation you need to simplify your life, allowing your relationships to really bloom.

Mental Health

In addition to the physical health benefits of decluttering, we can count a great deal of mental health benefits. Eventually, when we are surrounded by belongings, our brains begin to play a trick on us. At first we may notice that things feel a little cluttered, but then we begin not even to see our mess. It's a natural part of the way the brain works. Things that are constantly around us fade into the background, much like we hear the hum of the air conditioner or fan as soon as we turn it on, but then later our brains tune it out. My mom notes that one of the reasons she likes fresh-cut flowers in a vase nearby once in a while is because they are new and temporary, so her brain takes note and she gets an extra dose of pleasure from her surroundings.

Our brains tune out the clutter in our homes. We may not even be aware that this clutter is causing us to feel heavy, depressed, overwhelmed, stressed, or just a little claustrophobic. We may not be able to identify our excess belongings as a cause of these feelings because our stuff has been in our homes for so long that it's almost become invisible to us. "A trashy, cluttered, overstuffed house can breed depression. People don't realize it, but your surroundings do affect you. You need to let some light in, and breathe some space in," writes John Barker, an interviewee.

By getting rid of the excess, you may find yourself waking up with a new, more optimistic outlook on life. If you're familiar with Feng Shui, you know that the way you arrange your furniture and the cleanliness of your home can lead to better energy. Decluttering may allow you to see creative new possibilities in the space around you, and in the wider world, leading to improved mental health.

Financial Health

In 2008, Adam Baker of *ManvsDebt.com* and his family found themselves massively in debt, so they decided to go minimal. This has dramatically transformed their financial picture. They've been able to pay off $18,000 in consumer debt after selling everything they own and rethinking their lifestyle. At a time when everyone is thinking about the state of the economy and trying to find ways to make their money go a little bit further, embracing a minimalist lifestyle could not be a better remedy for a less-than-ideal personal financial situation. This is because, as a minimalist, you won't spend as much money as you did before. You'll think twice before every purchase and only let something into your home if it's going to truly improve your quality of life.

According to an *EconomyWatch.com* article by Liz Zuliani that references data from *Money-zine.com* and *HoffmanBrinker.com*, the total amount of consumer debt in the U.S. in 2010 was almost 2.4

trillion dollars.[11] That comes out to about $7,800 in debt per person. Embracing a style of living where we only buy what we need with money that we actually have is important to our financial welfare. Adopting this attitude will save consumers from unnecessary and burdensome debt.

When my husband and I were planning our wedding, we knew that we wanted to spend a lot of time traveling during our first year of marriage. We sold or gave away much of what we owned. We realized that people would want to give us wedding gifts, things for the home, a home we were about to give up for a traveling lifestyle. We asked our wedding guests to kindly donate to our travel fund in lieu of giving gifts, and most of them complied with generosity. These two decisions, to sell our things and to ask for monetary wedding gifts, helped our newlywed financial picture tremendously. As you pursue the process of going through your belongings, you'll likely sell some of your unneeded items too. You can have a garage sale, a yard sale, a sale via *Craigslist*, or you can set up auctions for your smaller or more valuable items on *eBay*. I recommend only selling small, valuable items on *eBay* because it's not worth the time, hassle, and shipping expense for bulky or inexpensive items.

In an August 2012 blog post for *The New York Times,* entitled "You Probably Have Too Much Stuff," certified planner Carl

11   Liz Zuliani, "A Dozen Alarming Consumer Debt Statistics, Economy Watch, May 21, 2011,http://www.economywatch.com/economy-business-and-finance-news/a-dozen-alarming-consumer-debt-statistics.21-05.html.

Richards writes about realizing that holding on to things he didn't need was costing him. "When we hold on to stuff we no longer want or use, it does indeed cost us something more, if only in the time spent organizing and contemplating it. I can't tell you how many times I've thought about getting rid of that tie, for instance, and every time I went to choose a shirt for the day, I would think about the few that no longer fit,"[12] he writes. Richards' more moderate simplifying process was inspired by Andrew Hyde, who made the news in 2010 when he declared that he only owned 15 items.

Once you begin divesting yourself of excess belongings, you will notice an abundance of space in your home. You may also notice that when you have space, your instinct is to fill it. For this reason, you may consider downsizing to a smaller home. In Italy and many European countries, people live by necessity and by choice in smaller homes and apartments than we do in the U.S. Smaller homes in these European countries help create a culture where people leave home for their leisure activities, perhaps going for walks in the evening to their nearby sidewalk café where they develop a healthy community of social connections in their neighborhood. By having a smaller home, we are less tempted to buy things we don't need. Along with lower mortgage payments or rent and lower utilities bills, there's less likelihood that we will allow ourselves what Claire Wolf, in an article entitled "The Art of Living in Small Spaces,"

12   Carl Richards, "You Probably Have Too Much Stuff," *The New York Times*, August 13, 2012, http://bucks.blogs.nytimes.com/2012/08/13/you-probably-have-too-much-stuff/.

calls "mad acquisition binges." As you plan your life around what's important to you rather than what's conventional, you might choose to downsize to a smaller home that costs the same as your previous home, but its proximity to an urban center, coastline, or park that you love means less time wasted in the car and less money spent on gas. Sarah Susanka's book *The Not So Big House: A Blueprint for the Way We Really Live* might be a useful guide as you educate yourself about the possibility of having a richer, less financially draining life in a smaller, well-designed, well-built space.

Improved financial health may be one of the most compelling reasons for many to declutter and live a less consumerist lifestyle. But I'd like to emphasize that selling individual items is not where our financial value is going to come from. Most of the value is going to come from time we save. Time we save not cleaning a house that's too big for us. Time we save that would otherwise be spent repairing, moving, organizing, and just thinking about our belongings. This time has financial value, and it also has value to your happiness and quality of life. The bottom line is: time is money. Time is also your life. Spend it wisely, preferably not in daily contemplation of those shirts that you really should get around to getting rid of.

Healthier Relationships

We've already talked about how making time for relationships can increase your joy. Let's go into a bit more detail here about how simplifying can lead to healthier relationships that in turn increase our happiness. Our stuff so often can become a barrier: between us and the people that we care about, between us and new, exciting friendships and relationships, between us and the world. Think about a hoarder who surrounds him or herself with clutter: old newspapers, magazines, coffee cans, and extra furniture. This person builds a wall of stuff that keeps the world out.

Sometimes we need to clear the way for a new relationship to bloom. As in Cheri Cruden's case from the last chapter, releasing belongings that we've held onto that might be associated with past pain can be very healthy for our current relationships. The key to successful relationships is being present. When we hold on to things that are associated with unpleasant or very nostalgic, emotional past events, those things act as an anchor dragging us down into the deep water of the past, instead of allowing us to float buoyantly in the present of our current relationships. Also, if your home is completely packed, it's going to be darker and less pleasant for visitors and for you. That may put a damper on your social life.

The benefits of minimalist living are, of course, all connected. Reaping financial benefits from downsizing your home can release stress and pressure in a marriage. Having more space in your home to pursue the way you really live your life and the things that you really enjoy can enhance a relationship. Instead of clambering over piles of stuff to get to and enjoy each other, you can literally or metaphorically dance in the new open space you will create.

Speaking of creating, minimalist living can have an energizing effect on your creativity. Let's find out how in the next chapter.

CHAPTER FOUR

For Creativity

"Creativity is subtraction." — Austin Kleon

You know the fantasy. You enter a room, and a sense of peaceful, creative energy envelops you. It's a calm place, with blank surfaces for writing, painting, or crafting. There's plenty of light. All the tools you need are available, organized, clean, and in places that make sense to you and to anyone else who needs to access them. Perhaps you got this fantasy from a magazine image or from visiting an artist's studio or friend's home. Maybe you thought that wasn't possible for you, with the way things get lost and the way supplies and clutter proliferate lustily. But it's achievable for you. You're going to learn the tools – both expected and unexpected – that will help you turn your clutter zones into spaces where your creativity can flourish, whether you need to be creative for work or play or both. If a more creative life is one of your goals, then decluttering your home, schedule, and thoughts is vital. I believe that we are all creators. We create art, relationships, products, and experiences. We even create our own bodies by what food we put in them and how we train and exercise them. We create our emotions and moods by what thoughts we choose to dwell on. Everyone is creative. Whether we think of ourselves as creative or not, we all create. Sometimes we create consciously, such as when writing a book, and sometimes unconsciously, such as when we engage in a bout of negative thinking, creating a bad mood for ourselves.

To consciously create requires room in our home, office or studio. Even more than room, we need time in our schedules. And, most importantly, we need to let go of the thoughts that do not serve us. We need to declutter our mental space from the thoughts that hold us back from our highest creative potential.

Making Room

I took a survey of creative people to find out about their biggest frustrations regarding clutter in their homes, studios and offices. These are some of their responses on the topic of clutter and creativity:

"[I am frustrated by] having new items purchased and brought into the house without making the effort to first dispense with things we don't need. Knowing that I should dispose of things responsibly, but not having sufficient priorities to the task to research where and how. I hate throwing things into the landfill that could be sent somewhere more usefully. Clutter is often the outcome of creative effort. My desk is always messiest when I have a lot of work on. The workshop too, but sweeping through and setting things right is essential, or I can't find anything, nor accomplish anything.

"[Clutter] distracts me and makes me feel like a worthless individual. I can't get anything done until I clean it up."

"[I'm frustrated when] my cleaning lady puts things in the wrong place all the time. My (paper) files aren't in order because we've moved so often and don't have enough file space, and when I need to find something, often I can't. If it's something crucial or time-dependent, I get anxious about it, usually at 2 in the morning or so. Half my books are still in storage and the rest aren't in order, which makes me feel disorganized.

"[I'm frustrated that clutter] makes me look disorganized even when I'm not. [Yet] it's sometimes difficult to see everything I have when it's put away, which stops me from making connections. Sometimes one type of clutter (junk mail, etc) gets mixed in with another (yarn, painting things) and then it is hard to find things.

"Clutter is visual noise that prevents you from seeing clearly. It is visual agitation, or visual perturbation. It takes subconscious effort to ignore clutter, and this effort builds stress. The work environment itself is no less a work of art than the subject matter. It is the container, the birthplace, the medium through which other things happen. The subconscious sometimes allows clutter to develop so that creativity cannot be attempted, out of fear of failure, or through a lack of genuine interest in being creative. Being free of clutter is probably most important during the phase when decisions over creative objectives are being made."

"I can't start anything productive without first clearing away the clutter in my work space, living area, and mind."

"I cannot think clearly when a space is cluttered. I need a blank exterior environment so I can hear my interior world."

"Clutter, for me, is like creative block because if it's not tidy, that sits in the back of my mind as a stressor and hinders my progress. I often find an outside source for creative outlet but would prefer my home."

"[Clutter makes me feel] irritable and therefore unable to be productive and creative."

"I have trouble concentrating on my writing when the house is cluttered - I keep thinking, 'I should be working on this mess...'"

Clearly, for many, clutter is an obstacle to creativity.

This may not be the case for you, however. When decluttering your space think first about what you want out of an ideal workspace. I interviewed writer-poet Austin Kleon regarding his workspace, clutter, and organization, and he had this to say:

I like a lot of light, which is easy to come by in Texas. I like to have a lot of books around and I like to have walls where I can pin up pieces of inspiration. I've worked in the same environment for over half a decade now — I have a little office at the landing of the stairs in our townhouse. There's no door, so it can sometimes be hard to concentrate and create boundaries between living and working, but then again, since I watch my son part time, there really isn't much boundary between my life and work right now anyways. The minute my son goes down for a nap, I'm back at the desk working.

[...]

One thing I talk about in Steal Like An Artist *is having separate analog and digital desks. The analog desk is a distraction-free zone where you keep pens and paper. The digital desk is where everything electronic goes. I've found this breakdown has really helped me get into different modes with my work — the analog desk is where I get raw ideas and experiment and play, and the digital desk is where I do a lot of the executing of ideas — scanning artwork, Photoshopping, typing, sending emails, etc. The other day my wife sent me the Wikipedia link for "mise en place" which is a French cooking term that roughly translates to "everything in its right place." In professional kitchens, they'll have all the ingredients prepared and ready to go before they do the cooking. As messy as my office is, there are paths cleared to the work space, and everything's ready to go — I keep my drawing desk clear with a healthy supply of newspapers and markers, and I keep my laptop ready and waiting for me to sit down and immediately start writing.*

In addition to the creative souls who feel stymied, distracted, or irritated by clutter, there are those who find being surrounded by diverse visual stimuli (AKA clutter) creatively inspiring.

Survey respondents who felt this way about clutter said things like:

"[Clutter] doesn't bother me very much. I make connections between materials that otherwise would not be available to me when I see a lot of things on my desk."

"[Clutter makes me feel like] a bit of a cliché, free, chaotic. This is good."

Kleon says regarding his "messy" work space, "While my work is subtractive, my studio space is additive – when I'm really deep into a project like I am right now, I like to really surround myself with inspiration and piles of junk. I like to have everything out where I can see it while I'm working. There's a great line from Ellen Ullman in Close to the Machine: "The disorder of the desk, the floor; the yellow Post-it notes everywhere; the whiteboards covered with scrawl: all this is the outward manifestation of the messiness of human thought.' I'm not a big 'things organized neatly' guy; I'm more of a "things spread out everywhere" guy."

You can still be a minimalist if you share Kleon's attitude towards creativity and clutter. If you prefer to work in an environment that's filled with "the outward manifestation of the messiness of human thought," then your minimalist focus will be on decluttering your time and your thoughts so you create.

Making Time

When I lived in Los Angeles as an aspiring screenwriter, many of my friends were also writers who had day jobs. During our off hours, we would spend time chipping away at our latest screenplays in the hopes of improving our craft and, eventually, seeing our name under "written by" on the screen in a sold-out movie theater. Any time this group of friends would get together, there would always be a few who couldn't make it because they were at home writing. "____ is writing tonight" was such a ubiquitous excuse that it became a joke and a euphemism for just about any other excuse someone could have for not showing up at a social event.

Even though once in a while "I have to write tonight," was an excuse, the idea of clearing time for creativity is a great one. One key to clearing time in your schedule for creativity is to learn to use these two phrases:

1. No thank you.

2. Maybe — I'll think about it.

I notice that creative and productive people have a lot of passion about a wide variety of topics and projects. That passion is wonderful, but it can lead to waste and burnout if it's not focused on three projects or fewer at any given time. If you commit to projects, requests, and ideas willy-nilly, there will be one of two possible outcomes. The first is that you will forget, flake out, or drop the ball on some of these projects. That leads to you letting yourself down, or disappointing others if it was a team project. The second potential outcome, if you carry out all of your projects and commitments while continuing to pile on more, is that you will feel exhausted, drained, too-busy, bored, unfulfilled, trapped, and possibly resentful. So many of us are used to pleasing others at the cost of nurturing our own creativity. We agree to take part in too many activities and projects. That's why, no matter how excited you are about a new idea, learning to say "no" or "maybe" is pivotal to living a peaceful, joyful, creative life as a minimalist.

Once it becomes easy to say "maybe," you can make the gradual adjustment to being a person who agreeably says "no" all the time. Practice aloud when you're alone:

"No thank you. I have to paint."

"No thank you. I will be practicing the ukulele at that time."

"No thank you. I will be creating my six-pack abs then."

Of course, if it's something you truly want to do, if every cell in your body is screaming, "Yes! You must do this!" then, by all means, say "maybe." Fit this advice to your personality. If it's rare for you to feel your entire being telling you that you must do something, then congratulations, you already have a minimalist filter. By all means, say yes if you know you truly want to do something. But if "A million times yes!" is your routine response, learn to say "no," or "maybe" more frequently so that you can take time to nurture your creative spirit.

Creating Mental Space

A friend shared a beautiful metaphor with me about decluttering your mental space. We talked a little about this in Chapter Two, but I'd like to go into more detail here. Imagine your brain as a beautiful, calm harbor. You are the harbor master, so you can choose what ships can anchor in the harbor. You can't control which ships sail by, but you can choose not to let certain ships into the harbor.

Just like you choose what goes into your home and what goes into your schedule, you can choose what thoughts you allow to enter your harbor. You may not be able to keep certain thoughts from flitting by, but you can decide not to entertain certain thoughts. By choosing your thoughts and intentions carefully, you create a more peaceful inner life, a life that is more joyful and creative.

So what thoughts are the enemies of creativity and what to do about them? The number one damaging thought I come across as a coach is self doubt. Lack of confidence to move forward with one's ideas is a creativity killer. Austin Kleon recommends decluttering "that fearful editor in your brain that tells you you're not good enough. Everybody has one. I've found that meditation helps a lot."

The reason meditation helps with this very personal, internal decluttering process is that it trains you to be mindful, or to keep your thoughts actively present in the now. When you're mindful, you're fully experiencing your life, actions, emotions, and sensations as they are in this moment. Creating mental white space that allows our imagination to blossom isn't as easy as pitching out what we don't need. That method works with our space and our time, but it doesn't work in our minds. That's because in the very act of trying to get rid of a thought, we can't help but focus on that thought! That outcome is the opposite of our goal.

Instead of trying *not* to think about something, bring your attention to the moment you're in. If you want to paint a portrait, get into the process of painting as soon as possible. Then keep your attention focused on the act of painting itself. To go back to the harbor metaphor, staying present keeps your harbor full of peaceful ships, so the pirate ships of self-doubt can see that there is no room for them and keep sailing to somewhere else.

Minimalism as a Creativity Booster

Minimalism itself can fuel creativity. Maintaining this lifestyle can boost the imagination by providing limits and structure to the way you design your home and time. Bea Johnson of the *Zero Waste Home* blog has created beautiful and imaginative solutions in her household's quest to create very little trash each year. She says, "My creativity is fed by finding alternatives for zero waste." Even if you don't want to change your lifestyle as radically as the Johnsons did, embracing a more moderate attitude toward consuming will still challenge your thinking and stoke your creativity.

CHAPTER FIVE

Facing Resistance

"Resistance is futile."— The Borg in *Star Trek*

Now that we've talked about how minimalist living can bring you joy, health, and creativity, let's talk about some resistance you might be facing before we dig in to the nuts-and-bolts of exactly how to declutter in the next chapter. Generally speaking, there are two main categories of resistance to becoming a minimalist: internal and external.

Internal Resistance

If you've found yourself procrastinating on simplifying, you may be harboring some deep-seated fears of going through everything. That's normal and natural, because it will mean a big change in your surroundings and possibly your life. You are right to be afraid of change, because change often brings unpredictable outcomes. But fear is the best teacher when it is faced head on and interviewed for the lessons it has to give. That's right; you're going to interview your fear.

Before we wade into the high weeds of decluttering, I'd like to invite you into a journey with your subconscious mind. This guided journey is inspired by the work and teachings of philosopher and metaphysician Catherine Collautt, Ph.D.

The following exercise will be especially helpful for you if you've wanted to declutter for a long time, but no matter how much you desire and plan for it, things just keep getting in the way. Let's do this exercise together; even if it seems a little "woo-woo," you might be surprised at the outcome.

Ask your fear what there is to be afraid of, and listen compassionately to the answers, perhaps even writing them down. Go ahead, say to your fear "What are you afraid of?"

Listen to the answers. As an example, you might find that you're afraid that you will get rid of something that you need or want later, that the process of editing your belongings will cause injury or psychological stress, or that you will work hard to clean out your home, and then it will simply fill back up. Are you afraid you won't be able to maintain your hard work?

Perhaps you're afraid that you'll be forced to confront the past in a way that is painful. You might find old projects that remind you of old, long-abandoned goals or dreams. Perhaps you'll feel a sense of failure or anxiety as you contemplate things you know you shouldn't have spent money on. An interviewee wrote, "When you get rid of something you have to acknowledge that the dream is dead and not acted upon, that the task is hopelessly beyond due and now irrelevant due to inaction, or that the money truly was wasted and there is nothing you can do to recover from the bad decision."

Facing these fears can be the most draining, exhausting, and demoralizing part of the entire decluttering process. Be gentle and loving with yourself, and rather than blaming yourself for anything, imagine what you'd say to a friend in the same situation. Say that to yourself. You'll push through to the other side, and you'll feel a new sense of truly owning and facing up to your life as it really is. Hopefully, no matter what the past contains, you'll appreciate yourself for facing up to it and creating a better present for yourself. It's what you do today that makes you into who you'll be tomorrow.

Whatever your fears are, write them down or simply say them out loud. Get them out of your head in some way. Write down even the ones that you don't understand or the ones that seem unrelated to the issue. Isn't it a relief to face them and see clearly what you're dealing with?

And now we can deal with each fear individually.

For each fear, promise yourself that you're going to do your best not to let that happen (if it's a fear about the future) or forgive yourself and seek forgiveness from others (if it's something you regret about the past). Our fears can be like children – not fully rational, but certainly able to spoil a party if they need attention. Give your fears gentle attention and reassure them that you understand and you commit to making sure that you will address them.

I know this process can seem a little unusual, but what we are doing here is getting our subconscious mind partnered fully with our conscious mind, goals and desires.

To complete the fear-quenching process, find examples of people who keep their home in the way that you would like to despite the obstacles. Remind yourself of these people as you go through the decluttering process.

Now that we've dealt with our individual fears, let's tackle two common concerns that many folks have about lightening their load.

What If I Need It

"It's fine for the very wealthy to get rid of things with abandon," you might say. "But what about normal people on a budget? I can't just go out and buy anything I might need on a whim. I'd much rather have it in storage in case I need it."

It's a good point and a common fear. First of all, we are going to do our best not to get rid of things that we really need. Therefore, there's no need to be afraid that we'll get rid of something vital.

Secondly, as we discussed in Chapter Three, paring down can have a positive effect on your budget, meaning that you might indeed have the money to buy or rent something that you want later.

Storing things is fine – as long as we know what we have and we use and enjoy those things. Storing things because we might need them someday usually results in forgetting what we have and buying a new version of the thing anyway. When things are in storage, they become outdated. Clothes are a great example of this. Even though fashions come back every 20-30 years, they usually return with tweaks and modern updates that make the actual past fashions inherit a dated look.

Remember that when you have stuff, you have to:

- Unpack it

- Set it up

- Put it away

- Clean it

- Maintain it

- Fix it when it gets broken

- Update it

- Upgrade it

- Throw it out, recycle it, sell it, or give it away

Each of these steps takes time, time you can also spend making money, if you so choose. So in a way, keeping extra stuff is often not a wise financial choice, although that is not always intuitive unless you really consider that time is money. Time is all we ever really have.

Still afraid of giving up something that you'll miss? Look at your community. Your friends might like some of your things. Even if they too are minimalists, it's likely that they've been wanting to try a new hobby – camping, for instance, and it just so happens that you haven't camped in years and you want to get rid of your gear. In this scenario, your wannabe camping friends get your camping gear as a free gift. However, they are still your friends, which means that one day, if you should ever want to go camping, you can probably borrow your paraphernalia back from them. If it's books you want to off-load but are afraid you'll miss, your community library might welcome them. Small, local libraries will shelve most of the books you donate, allowing you to check them out later. If you're having a hard time parting with something, looking to your community is a comforting option.

The Latest Gadgets

Let's face it - new stuff is fun. Inventors are constantly solving the really annoying problems of life by creating new products. But let's keep in mind that inventors are also solving problems that don't actually exist. Have you ever flipped through the pages of *Sky Mall* magazine on an airplane? It's full of hilarious examples of products with such niche markets I can't help wonder if the niche is empty. For example, who needs a life size hanging chimp sculpture? But I'll admit that I like window shopping and I can see the appeal of a beautiful new mitten-scarf set. I'm here to tell you that you can still enjoy the new gadgets and luxury items on Oprah's List of Favorite Things. Just don't buy anything that you aren't going to use. And before you buy, declutter one item that you haven't used in a while. And finally, if you do buy something that you don't end up using, let it go on to a new home. In time, you may find that while you own fewer things, those that you do own are of a higher quality, and more luxurious. This is a result of planning your purchases and having more money to spend now that you're buying less. This kind of shopping can be more fun than impulse buying because you can take time to enjoy the process and save up for high quality purchases.

External Resistance

It's true that more often than not other people can be the biggest obstacle to our decluttering dreams. Husbands, wives, family, friends, and anyone else who happens to hang around your space with regularity can certainly mess with plans for becoming a minimalist. A couple of people who took my survey about clutter mentioned their frustrations with other people:

"My partner with whom I live does not share equally in keeping our place organized and tidy. He causes most of the clutter and sometimes I feel like a maid!"

"I like having little things around, they inspire me to live in the small spaces and take little things seriously, but straight clutter, or someone else's stuff makes me anxious."

Minimalism in a Marriage

Ideally, you get your spouse or significant other completely on board with the ideas in this book, and you go merrily on your way to minimalist living. However, I'm aware that the ideal doesn't always happen in real life. If your significant other doesn't seem too keen on simplifying, first see if he or she is open to reading this book. If not, simply talk to him or her about your desires to feel less stressed about your belongings. It's likely your spouse will agree, but he or she might have fears or concerns about how the paring down will happen.

It can also help to know if you're married to or living with a collector or a purger. These two appellations were dreamed up by aunt, a purger from birth. Collectors are born pack rats, people who love to gather treasures and keep them in boxes, on shelves, or displayed in cases. Purgers are people who feel burdened by knickknacks and thinking about their stuff. They willingly, periodically, and often methodically sort through every room in their house to get rid of the old so they can make room for the new – whether that is new stuff, new space, new people, or new dreams.

Collectors love nostalgia, the energy associated with certain belongings, reminders of lovely memories, and thinking fondly about the past. Purgers are hooked on optimism, fresh starts, and dreams for the future.

Collectors can change to purgers, or at least to less-stuff-oriented collectors. This change is usually activated by a dramatic life event. I used to be a collector, and then most of my sentimental items were destroyed in a fire. Today, although I still love a good stroll down memory lane, I am more oriented toward valuing my dreams for the future rather than my collections, memorabilia, and sentimental items.

Identifying which descriptor you and your partner each lean toward can help you understand issues and different opinions on how, and if, you should simplify your lifestyle. The member of the household who wields responsibility for the majority of the housekeeping is usually the personality that prevails upon the stuff situation. In other words, if a collector is the person mainly in charge of housekeeping, then the home will probably have a few too many belongings stored in it. If a purger is responsible for the majority of housekeeping and decoration, it will be more likely to be a minimalist space. Two collectors married to each other can change their ways, but it takes a mighty wind. A purger and a collector need to be very careful to get on the same page and reach an understanding of how the simplification process will be undertaken. Two purgers married to each other can just enjoy the ride as they joyfully pitch out anything (if there is anything) that has come to rest in the attic or basement over the years.

In any case, approaching minimalism as a couple or a family takes an extra step of cooperation and understanding. Admit who is going to be more enthused about the project and who is going to take some time to get used to a more pared down life. Communication, always central to any kind of team effort, is quite essential to a successful change in lifestyle and attitude about consumerism within a family.

Leo Babauta of ZenHabits spotlighted a student, Rick, who took his Clutterfree course. Rick wrote about the process and the importance of setting ground rules with his significant other:

> *Since we were both going to be dealing with issues that arose as we let things go, we decided it was important to set*

some ground rules. Our most important rule – each of us had to deal with our own stuff. I would not force or press her to get rid of anything that was 'hers.' And she would not press me to get rid of anything that was 'mine.' For the many things that are joint property, whoever had the stronger emotional attachment to the item got to decide what to do with it. We promised each other that the most we would ever do to question the decision to keep any particular item is to pick it up, look at the other person and say, 'Seriously?!?' then walk away. We've kept to these rules pretty well so far.

You may encounter stiff resistance from your significant other about any lifestyle changes. In this case, just bringing up the subject of minimalism can be met with suspicion or misunderstanding. Stop and take a different tactic. Courtney Carver of BeMoreWithLess.com recommends daydreaming with your spouse.[13] What goals and dreams do you share? Traveling? Getting out of debt? Buying a boat? Often simplifying can be a part of that vision your spouse might not see unless he or she is concurrently feeling the compelling emotion of the shared dream.

If you simply can't get your spouse or other family members on board with your decluttering plan, then pursue minimalism in your own domains within your home. Apply what you're learning to your spaces, your hobbies, your time, and your inner life. Once your

13   Courtney Carver, "When Your Spouse Isn't Simple," http://bemorewithless.com/2011/when-your-spouse-isnt-simple/.

loved ones see the benefits you're creating in your life and the new space you're opening up, it's more likely they will want to join the party. If you've been married for a while, you know that you can't change your mate, but you can change your own behavior. Always value the relationship over minimalist living. If simplifying is causing damage to your relationship, stop and take a break. Done with patience, love, and a sense of humor, becoming a minimalist improves relationships.

For a beautiful example of a couple working in seemingly perfect harmony, check out MarriedWithLuggage.com. Warren and Betsy Talbot describe themselves as a "Recovering, 40-something, Type-A couple who learned that living large is not necessarily living well." After some health scares in the family, the Talbots, both 37 at the time, asked themselves, "If we knew we wouldn't make it to our 40th birthdays, what would we do differently right now?" That was in 2008. By the time their 40th birthdays rolled around, they had sold all of their belongings, saved "a mountain" of money, and begun a world-traveling adventure that continues today. The Talbots are inspiring; you too can get rid of your stuff and travel the world with your partner. Even more to the point, you can work together to create the lifestyle you want through embracing minimalism.

Decision Time

Individually if necessary, but preferably with your spouse or family, make a decision before you move on to the next few chapters, which are the "how-to declutter" portion of the book. Decide to become a minimalist and to define what minimalism means for your life and home. Once you have a definition, fulfill that vision. It's important that you create your vision before you begin so that you have something to guide you and inspire you in the process, and so you aren't tempted to change it along the way simply because it's easier to change your definition than to fulfill your original vision. We'll call this vision your Minimalist Mission Statement. Hold it as sacred to your home. This technique is also used by famous television organizer Peter Walsh. He begins work by asking his clients, "What's your vision for the life you want and the home you want?"

Use that question and the questions below to guide you as you think about or write down your answers. If you're looking at this with a significant other, please change each occurrence of "I" to "we" and "my" to "our" for the following questions:

- How do I want my home to look?

- How do I want my home to feel?

- How do I want my home to smell? (i.e., like freshly baked bread, coffee, candles, fresh air, etc.)

- How do I want my home to sound? (i.e., silent, music, a fountain, birds outside, wind chimes, conversation, laughter, etc.)

- What hobbies, activities, and creative work am I spending time on now?

- What hobbies, activities, and creative work do I desire to be spending my time on?

- How can I change my surroundings to reflect these desires?

- Is my home set up in a default or conventional way, or in a way that reflects my authentic, unique self?

- Do I have items stored away that I haven't looked at or used in over a year?

- Do I have things in plain sight that I haven't used or enjoyed in over a year?

- What is the purpose of my home and how can I change things to make my home fit its purpose as I define it?

- Do I have stuff stored at another location that I haven't accessed for at least one year?

- Am I storing things for other people?

- If so, do I have a plan for returning those items to people or a set date when they will pick them up?

- Am I saving supplies for a project that, honestly, I am never going to get to?

- In 1-3 sentences, my Minimalist Mission Statement for my home when this decluttering project is complete is:

Think of your hobbies, interests, passions, and perhaps even important relationships when you write your Minimalist Mission Statement. Here are some examples of Minimalist Mission Statements:

Our home is a place where we make our friends and family feel welcome. We always have delicious snacks and drinks on hand, and the kitchen is the center of it all, making our home smell like fresh bread, or just-baked artichoke dip. We love to show hospitality to our friends, making them feel comfortable, safe, and loved.

My home is a haven where I work in front of a window with an inspiring view. The house smells like the fresh air that comes in from the hills when I open all the big windows. I don't have much furniture because I like to dance in my open living room for exercise. My friends don't mind my lack of furniture; they come over and casually sit on the kitchen counter, laughing and chatting, maybe even dancing, and then we go out to a coffee shop to get comfortable.

We love to be out, giving to our community. Outside, our home is surrounded by a well-tended garden, making our neighborhood look more beautiful. Inside, our home is one big workshop where we make crafts to give away and sell, and where we fix things for people who are not as ready with the drill and glue gun as we are.

And this is my Minimalist Mission statement:

My home is a heart-centered place where my family and friends feel welcome and loved. For me, minimalist living means keeping only what I actually use and enjoy on a regular or seasonal basis. Things I don't use and enjoy can go on to enrich someone else's life. I limit my sentimental items to one box so I can move without those things getting lost. The things that are important to my heart are people, not things.

Make your Minimalist Mission Statement a reflection of your uniqueness. It can be whatever you want it to be. Write it down and post it on a wall that you see all the time. Your Minimalist Mission Statement will be your guide going forward.

CHAPTER SIX

Begin Today

"Enough words have been exchanged; now at last let me see some deeds!" — *Goethe (*Faust I*)*

The best way to start simplifying is to get rid of one item right now. Even though you haven't finished this book or finished reading the advice and guidelines that will help with the process later, begin now.

Go ahead. I'll wait. Take five minutes or less and put something out by the curb or create a "give away" box and place one item in it.

Did you do that? Good.

What's that? You didn't? It's easy. I promise. And you'll feel really good once you come back to the book.

Come back once you've gotten rid of one thing that is taking up too much space in your life. Did you do it?

Great job!

Okay, now you've begun. You've done the hardest part. You acted boldly. Well done. Now we can move forward together. We've defined minimalism for ourselves, and considered all the wonderful things that living this way can bring to our lives. We faced the resistance, made a choice to become minimalists, created our own Minimalist Mission Statements, and have already begun. That wasn't too hard. Now let's get into the practical how-to part of this book and learn some great ways to make the next step – implementing our vision – a fun one.

Blazing and Gazing

We are out to kill stress by decluttering and simplifying in a careful, intentional way that honors our belongings and our homes.

There are a lot of ways to do this, but let's keep it simple. There are really only two main methods for creating new space in your home: the blaze method and the gaze method. Whether you blaze or gaze will depend on your personality and the specifics of your relationship to your stuff.

The Blaze Method

I named it the blaze method because at its most expedient, you simply imagine that a blazing fire nearby is going to burn down the home, room, drawer, or closet you're decluttering and you have only minutes to select the essential items. You keep those essentials, and dispose of the remainder without a second thought. It's "ripping the band-aid off" and can be rather painful in the short term, but blessedly quick. For some, blazing can be very appealing, but they are worried that this method is somehow irresponsible. I'm here to give you permission to blaze merrily along, if that's what you need. There's no rule that says you have to have an intimate knowledge of what you're getting rid of.

A variation on the blaze method is to select essential items from the area you're editing, and, instead of disposing of the rest immediately, putting it out of sight in boxes or closets for six months to a year. Within that time, you can fetch anything you wish you hadn't gotten rid of. After a few seasons have passed, you can get rid of the stuff, comfortable in the knowledge that you don't need anything in the boxes. However, the danger in the out of sight method is re-cluttering by regret and retrieval. If you sneak into the closet and select too many things to return to your home over time, you'll undo your work. Sometimes it's best to just get it out of the house, or make it truly unavailable, as soon as possible.

Leo Babauta of *ZenHabits.net* is a proponent of a type of blazing, which he refers to as the "Four Laws of Simplicity." Here they are in his words:

1. Collect everything in one place.

2. Choose the essential.

3. Eliminate the rest.

4. Organize the remaining stuff neatly and nicely.

The Gaze Method

So named because of the method's potential to allow us to gaze upon our treasures, letting each take us down memory lane, gazing can be a bit more agonizing and prolonged than blazing. However, it's more thorough, and arguably, less financially risky since blazing could lead to something valuable being thrown out without our noticing. Gazing takes discipline and certainly more time than blazing. Gazing can also be more emotionally painful, or troubling, for people who labor over the decision to keep or discard each little item. Sometimes it's better to decide quickly, as in the blaze method.

When I was a kid, I adored gazing. I'd clear off a shelf in my room and spend time looking at each item, remembering where I found it, or the person who gave it to me. Sometimes I'd even imagine giving the item to my future children, or I'd daydream and make up a story that the item played a central role in. This daydreaming was no doubt good for the development of my imagination and creativity, but I didn't need the mementos to do it.

In fact, daydreaming while looking at the shapes of clouds was even more fun and it got me outside.

If you choose the gazing method, have a defined plan and timeline that you stick to, because otherwise this method can steal truckloads of time out of your life. Also, while the blaze method can be undertaken more or less alone (although I don't recommend it), it is vital that you seek support if you decide on gazing. Without people to help keep you on track, it's more likely you'll get stuck somewhere in the quagmire of old memories and this could keep you from finishing.

Combining Methods

Do you remember from the last chapter if you're a purger or a collector? Purgers will be much more likely to blaze, while collectors will enjoy the gazing process. If a purger and a collector are working together, it is also possible to combine the two methods in one home, perhaps blazing certain junk drawers and gazing the treasure box under your bed. You may also find yourself feeling like employing a different method on a different day depending on your mood and how busy you're that day. Sometimes, when we find a drawer that is stuffed full of forgotten items, my husband says "We need to do a blaze-and-gaze." Combining methods is most realistic for couples who need to make sure they aren't throwing away each other's stuff.

Even if you'll be using a little of both methods, pick your favorite so you know which one you'll *mainly* be using. Go with the one that most excites you and gives you a sense of energy and openness, not the one that makes you feel dread or makes you want to procrastinate. Whatever method you choose, have fun with it. This whole process can be fun if you give yourself plenty of time and support.

Decluttering Area by Area

Now we'll go through each room in the house, each outdoor space, and any storage spaces. As we look at each area, we'll subdivide it into the smallest portions we need to in order for it to seem manageable. Some people will take bigger bites, and some will be more comfortable with nibbles. I find that doing a room per day seems doable but not overwhelming. You may want to go faster or slower. It will depend on the room and how much stuff is in it, and the nature of the belongings in the room. For example, to whom does the stuff belong? Is it extremely dusty, dirty, or dangerous to handle? It is valuable or will it all be trashed? Does any of it require special treatment such as old pharmaceuticals or electronics? Don't feel bad if you can do only one small area each day. My mom finds that she prefers to do one shelf or drawer per day, and she's a blazer. Go at your own pace.

As you approach each room, keep in mind your Minimalist Mission Statement. This will allow you to be discerning with what you keep and what you get rid of. For example, let's say you have a kitchen loaded with tools and gadgets, a closet stuffed with clothes and shoes, a sewing room filled with fabric scraps and notions, and a garage filled with seeds, soil, and gardening tools. Let's say that the exercise we did at the end of Chapter Three helped you realize that you haven't used the sewing supplies in a long time, and you don't really enjoy spending a long time selecting your outfit for the day each morning. In fact, you could care less about fashion. However, you've been enjoying gourmet cooking more and more, and you've taken a greater interest in growing your own vegetable garden in the back yard. In this case, while you'll still want to sort through your kitchen and gardening supplies for things you no longer need or use, it's likely that you'll keep most of those supplies. However, your realizations about sewing and fashion can free you to sell or give those supplies away as a set.

To save more space, consider replacing your hobbyist supplies with multi-purpose things. Multi-purpose and space-saving items exist in almost every category of household goods. From nesting bowls to nesting tables, it's easy to find minimalist substitutes for things you use infrequently. One creative strategy for space-saving items is to look for goods marketed for use in RVs, boats, or airplanes. Employ your favorite space-saving items and strategies for infrequently used things – after you've edited out the bulk of the things in that category.

Items for Use, Pleasure, or Meaning

Decide on your first room or section of a room. Make it small and easy, perhaps a drawer or one shelf. If you have selected the blaze method for this section, then blaze on through. Select the essentials and put the rest in a bag or box for sorting, which we'll discuss in just a moment.

If you have chosen the gaze method, you're going to ask yourself a set of questions about each item:

- Is this something that adds pleasure in the form of beauty or sensual enjoyment to my life?

- Is this useful to me in my daily life? My weekly life? My monthly or yearly life?

- Is this something that adds meaning to my life?

If the answer to all three questions is "yes," then it's probably an essential item.

Everything in our homes should be either useful, meaningful, or pleasurable, and preferably all three. Some organizing experts use the term "beautiful" instead of pleasurable, but I wanted to widen the concept. Beauty brings pleasure, but connotes only pleasure to sight – just one of many senses. The word "pleasurable" can describe something that pleases the sense of smell, touch, or hearing. Asking "does this item bring me pleasure?" can keep us from getting rid of something that isn't necessarily an aesthetic marvel, but still adds a great deal to our daily life.

"Useful" refers to the item's functionality in our life. Does it serve a utilitarian purpose? Useful items are the most likely to be those that we use daily or weekly. Examples of these items are a computer, a laundry machine, and a can opener. It's unlikely that these are your most beautiful items, but if you're lucky and selective, form and function sometimes find their way together in useful items.

Meaningful items are the trickiest territory because "meaning" is different for everyone. The kind of items we are referring to when we say "meaningful" are cherished family heirlooms, beloved gifts, and anything else that contributes to a sense of heritage, memory, connection, or continuity with the past. Meaningful items are more than just sentimental items. Some people can get sentimental about anything: the wine cork from dinner last night; the heart-shaped box that came with the Valentine's Day chocolates; every item previously owned by a deceased relative; the fuzzy green sock that lost its mate; and the list goes on. If I've just described you, know that I can relate. I don't mean to undervalue our tender emotions and nostalgia. Having strong emotional associations makes life richer and makes relationships deeper and more meaningful. Simply acknowledge that just because something brings up strong emotions or memories doesn't mean you have to keep it.

There are ways to keep the emotional heart of an object as well as its connection to the past without having to keep the thing itself. Instead of keeping everything that has sentimental value, keep only the things – often they will be symbols of certain time periods or accomplishments – that truly have the deepest meaning to you and provide you with joy when you see them. Why keep things around that make you feel sad, guilty, stressed, resentful, bitter, or inadequate? Take control of the emotional energy around you by carefully selecting meaningful items to have on display.

Analyze exactly how your meaningful items make you feel. If there are strains of negative emotions within an item, get rid of it. For some reason I kept a letter from an old romantic interest for a long time. Things didn't work out, and he poured out his broken heart into the letter. Reading it made me feel guilty and sad. Yet I kept it for years, out of guilt for unintentionally hurting him and to remind myself how important it was to be careful with peoples' hearts. I would re-read it, want to throw it away, and keep it for some reason, unable to let go and forgive myself. Finally, I realized that I was only torturing myself, and got rid of it. Don't hold onto things to feel guilty, teach yourself a lesson, or remember past pain. If you felt the pain, the lesson got in – don't worry about that. If you hurt someone, ask forgiveness, try to make things right, forgive yourself, and move on.

Life is too short to spend time agonizing over regrets. The space you spend doing that is waiting to be free. Let go of the emotional and spiritual clutter along with the physical clutter. Have the courage to be self-serving with your possessions. They are yours, so allow them to serve up warm, nourishing, soothing, energetic, or positive feelings like love, joy, peace, respect, excitement, and pride. It takes courage to let go before you're assured of positive feelings to replace the negative ones. But you will be the one to design your home so that it reminds you of the positive in your life and what makes you feel good. Have faith in your ability to do so.

Here are some more questions to keep in mind to guide you in your editing process. You don't have to ask these questions about every item, but having them in the back of your mind will help:

- How did I acquire this item?

- Am I afraid of forgetting something or someone if I get rid of this thing?

- Is there any guilt associated with getting rid of this item? Why?

- Am I afraid of hurting someone's feelings if I get rid of this?

- If this item were broken or was stolen, would I feel a bit relieved?

Gifts

Disposing of gifts that we no longer like – or never liked, for that matter – is a notoriously tricky topic. What if the giver should ask about the gift? Is there a time allowance for how long something should be kept before it's acceptable to let it enhance someone else's life?

When you receive a gift – whether you like it or think it's hideous – you of course acknowledge the giver and express your gratitude. It really is the thought, not the gift, that counts. The relationship with the giver is what is important. Most people won't ask or follow up about gifts – and that is wise.

I once gave a gift and made the mistake of asking about it later. The gift was something that I really liked, and I had almost kept it for myself after I bought it. After giving it to my friend, I realized she never used it. So I asked her if she liked it, and if she didn't, could I borrow it once in a while or take it off her hands completely.

I should have simply never mentioned it again. My questions led to an awkward exchange because she was far too polite to admit that she didn't like it, or whatever the case was. What I learned is that most people are too polite to admit any reservations whatsoever about a gift. I have certainly white lied about how I feel about a gift. So, in case you have a friend who makes the same mistake I did and inquires later about a gift, simply know how you're going to respond. Never keep something just in case someone asks about a gift or to preserve someone's feelings. Instead, choose your strategy: complete honesty; a big fat white lie; or, preferably, the truth blunted with kindness. Most people understand that it's not possible to keep every item ever given to them.

Another measure you can take to insure yourself against follow-up questions about the gift is to wear, use, or display your gift at least once. Take a photo and email it to the giver, or hand write a note of gratitude. In addition to providing insurance against nosy follow-up questions, written acknowledgment is simply classy behavior. Once you express gratitude, then do as your heart desires with the gift, whether it be treasuring it forever or taking it to a charity.

Editing

Throughout this process, remember the value that editing can have for you. As with everything in life, there's as much art to what is left out as to what is put in. Don't underestimate how much energy and attention each thing you own takes from your life on a daily basis. For example, remember Carl Richards from Chapter Two? He's someone who would (and did, presumably) benefit from getting rid of the shirts that no longer fit him. To take it one step further, he could minimize his wardrobe even more, wearing a "uniform" of his choice every day. No one will care about his repeat outfits, and if they do, they are probably the sort of unpleasant people he wouldn't want to be around anyway. Plus he'll be too busy to worry about them; he'll be pursuing his actual interests and goals with the time and mental energy he's saving himself each morning. My parents have a friend who, after they complimented him on his appearance, told them that one day he'd simply decided to wear only what he felt handsome, sharp, and great in. If he put something on and it didn't fit the bill, he got rid of it.

On the flipside of this example, someone who has a passion for fashion or who takes great joy in dressing with variety each morning should keep his or her big closet and abundant choices.

Consider applying this concept of editing your choices in any area that you don't think much about, don't have a passion in, or would like to behave differently in. Here are some areas to get you started thinking about editing:

- Fashion

- Self-education (books, etc)

- Entertainment (movies, books, television, video games, music)

- Food

- Health

- Relaxation

- Personal grooming

- Outdoor furniture and accessories

- Fitness equipment

Editing for better habits and easier goal-fulfillment is one of the central tenets of this book. Make it easier on yourself to do what you love and to go after your desires. Put the tools and accessories for your favorite pastimes front and center. Make them the sacred heart of your home. Equally as important, get rid of stuff that distracts or that will sabotage your goals and dreams. Distractions include anything that you have only because it's conventional, because in the past you enjoyed it, or because you feel guilty about it – not because you currently use and enjoy it. Saboteurs include things that tempt you away from your goals, for example, junk food when you're watching your weight, or a television when you're trying to fill your free time with a more meaningful activity. Junk food, televisions, and other common saboteurs are all widely available in other people's homes, and well, just about everywhere. Should you miss them, they're easily found.

Area-Specific Advice

The process discussed here is effective for every area of the home, garage, and outdoor space. I'll add a few notes about specific spaces.

Closets

The usual advice, "If you haven't worn it in a year, get rid of it," is sound. I'd also suggest severely editing your closet down to a basic "uniform" if you don't enjoy thinking about fashion. A suggested uniform-like wardrobe is five shirts and three pairs of slacks for men, and 4 shirts, a dress, two pairs of slacks, and a skirt for women. Three pairs of shoes are usually sufficient for anyone, or perhaps four if you live in a snowy climate. Customize your wardrobe to your needs.

To help you simplify and declutter your closet, I've created a free, fully-customizable checklist for a 50-piece wardrobe that includes versions for both men and women. Visit the "free resources" section of SimpleLivingToolkit.com to find out more. You can use my checklist as a starting point to create your ideal wardrobe.

Garages, Attics, and Basements

These areas usually collect extra dust and clutter because they are out of sight from where most day-to-day living happens. Don't let yourself off the hook on these areas. Use extra care to protect your nose and eyes from dust.

Storage Units

Graham Hill notes that Americans have three times the amount of storage space in their homes and on their property today than they did fifty years ago. Yet despite the increased amount of storage, the personal storage industry is a 22 billion dollar, 2.2 billion square foot industry, reports Hill.[14] If you have things in a mini-storage unit, or several, ask yourself some hard questions about why it's there and how long it's been there. When are you going to use or get rid of the stuff? How much money have you spent on storage? What was your

14   Graham Hill, TED, "Less Stuff, More Happiness," March 2011, http://www.ted.com/talks/graham_hill_less_stuff_more_happiness.html?quote=1099.

plan when you put things in storage and have you stuck to your plan? If not, how can you follow through now? People with things in storage tend to leave them there for much longer than they intended and therefore spend more money than they were planning to. Monthly mini-storage rates in a big city can be more than utilities and a gym membership combined. Think hard before you ever put anything into storage. As Robert Frost wrote in his famous poem "The Road Not Taken,"

Oh, I kept the first for another day!

Yet knowing how way leads on to way,

I doubted if I should ever come back.

We make choices and move forward, rarely going back in life. Way leads on to way, and we don't always go back to our mini-storage units at all.

Just in case you aren't fully convinced about the downsides of putting your stuff in storage, I'll include the following portion of a Letter to the Editor written by an anonymous contributor. He's given me permission to reprint what he wrote after finding out that a mini-storage facility might be built near his San Francisco neighborhood:

Despair echoes loudest in the dark hallways of mini-storage facilities.

Almost every doorway opens into a sad story, each more tragic than the last.

The sadness hangs so heavily in the air that it creates a force as toxic as black mold.

It is where broken and incomplete people store pieces of their broken and

incomplete lives.

For many it is their address. Instead of an apartment or a dream home they once had, now a storage unit is all they can afford due to foreclosure.

These are the ones waiting at the gate when the mini-storage opens in the morning and the last to leave when it closes in the evening.

The key to their padlock is the only key they carry. The mini-storage

restroom becomes their bathroom, kitchen, and laundry.

When they do leave, many of them head to a shelter, a vehicle, a tent, or a cardboard box tucked in doorway of an alley a few blocks away.

These marginal citizens often scavenge the things that consumers cast off.

The treasures they cull from the trash end-up on blankets in sidewalk sales or in flea markets. The proceeds of these sales pay the cost

of their mini-storage rent. These are the people society cast off.

For others, the victims of job layoffs, evictions, divorces, illness, and

death, it is where the remnants of former lives reside, reminders of their

happier pasts, literally on cold storage for now. Some units contain a

deceased loved one's clothing and personal effects that heirs couldn't bear to throw away-tucked into a rented cubbyhole, overflowing with deferred grief.

These places are for people who are committed to not making a commitment.

They can't use it and they can't throw it away. They can't stay in a place

and they won't move away. They can't get on with their lives. They try to

maintain a past that doesn't exist anymore. They think paying rent to keep

unneeded items makes them more valuable.

The elderly on fixed incomes pay rent on memories with the hope they won't lose them. Instead of paying to hold on to pieces of their past they could be enjoying the present.

Souls tormented by the burden of their possessions roam the halls eerily

like ghosts. Many are ghosts of their former selves. Drug

addicts,

prostitutes, and the mentally ill seek asylum in their month-
to-month refuge from their hand-to-mouth existence. Thieves
and

prostitutes use their storage units to hide the loot they steal
or take in trade.

The proliferation of mini-storage units in a town is usually a
sign of its

decay. It tells of mass exodus, evictions, addiction, tragedy,
madness,

sickness, crime, incarceration, and death. It is a business that
supports and exploits the downward mobility of humanity. It
is a drain on a community that flushes directly to the bowels
of Hell.

If you were wondering, yes, the community kept the mini-storage unit out of the area.

Sort Later

As you go through your items, asking about the pleasure, use, and meaning each thing provides to your life, you'll be tempted to wonder what you're going to do with all the stuff you're getting rid of. Don't worry about that until the end of the room or section that you're working on. Instead, gather all the unneeded things – the stuff that doesn't serve you anymore – into a large box, bag, or designated space. This transitional box is a place where things can sit for a day or two during your editing process. Next, we'll talk about exactly what to do with all that extra stuff that is no longer serving you.

CHAPTER SEVEN

Creating a Fresh New Space

"Simplicity is the ultimate sophistication." – Leonardo da Vinci

Once you've treated a room to editing via the gazing or blazing process, you should have filled your transitional box or area. Perhaps you've even filled several bags or an entire room. The essential belongings that remain in the room are probably either scattered about on the floor or on whatever surface is available.

We can now turn our attention either to disposing of the items in the transitional box, or putting the room we've edited back into order. Let's put our attention on the room, first, since with a beautiful, clean, open room, we're more likely to stick to our intention of finding other homes for everything that we edited out.

Speaking of clean, now is a great time to scrub your freshly simplified space or have it professionally cleaned. Whether you clean it yourself or have a professional do it, make sure to use products free from indoor contaminants like volatile organic compounds (VOCs), especially if you have respiratory issues. Certain kinds of cleaning products can cause risks to your health. A study from the October 2007 issue of the *American Journal of Respiratory and Critical Care Medicine* identified 3,503 people who were asthma free at the beginning of the study. The results showed that 42% of the people who used cleaning sprays such as glass cleaners, furniture cleaners, and air fresheners over the course of the study experienced asthma symptoms. VOCs in common household cleaning products have been associated with asthma and implicated as carcinogens, reproductive toxins, hormone disruptors, and neurotoxins. To get you started on healthy cleaning, throw out any ammonia you have – or products that contain it. Ammonia is a nose, throat, and respiratory irritant. It can cause wheezing and shortness of breath; prolonged exposure can cause bronchitis.

Consider using the Environmental Working Group's guide to healthy cleaning to find out which products are safer. Don't trust labels on products at the store. Words like "green" or "natural" can be misleading because there are no standards that products must meet to put those words on a label. You can clean most surfaces in your home with soap, water, baking soda, and white vinegar, adding a few drops of your favorite essential oil for fragrance. Bonus points if you get rid of all the bottles of harsh and unhealthy chemical cleaners during your decluttering sessions.

Once you've cleaned and prepared your surfaces to hold your carefully selected remaining belongings, it's time to find a place for everything. You might find that your new Minimalist Mission Statement inspires you to move things around a little bit. Do so according to your vision for your home. In fact, this part is where the Minimalist Mission Statement is your best friend, so make sure to keep it handy.

Anything you have because it's beautiful or inspires joy should be displayed proudly, with good light and plenty of breathing room around it. The exception to this rule is collections of similar items, which often look better grouped together. Try to avoid curio cabinets unless they are lit from within and frequently cleaned. Otherwise, things tend to get lost in the dimness and dust of the interiors.

Everything else should be stored according to frequency of use. Store items based on how often you use them:

- Daily

- Weekly or Monthly

- Once or twice a year

Things you touch daily should be stored at eye or hand level, preferably out in the open. You should be able to access them almost effortlessly; doing so should not require leaning down or getting a stepping stool. Shelves, baskets, and countertops are ideal places to keep these items. Closets, cabinets, and drawers are less ideal, unless they are very easy to access.

Weekly or monthly-use items should also be stored in easy to access spots, but they can be out of sight, as long as they don't require using a stepping stool to access or moving other things to get to them.

Things you only use a couple of times a year or less can be stored in the least convenient storage places in your home, such as the attic or basement, under beds, or in high cabinets and shelves.

Think about it like this: daily use items should take zero "steps" to access. Opening drawers and cabinets and boxes each counts as a step. Ideally, weekly or monthly access items take only one step to access. And things you use really infrequently can take two or more steps to access (i.e., pulling down the ladder to go to the attic or crouching down and pulling a box out from under the bed.)

Finding a place for everything is vital, since even if you have only a few things, the place can still appear cluttered if things aren't pleasingly stashed. Yet perfection isn't the goal here, so don't stress about storing things. As you live in your new, minimalist space, you'll find yourself fine-tuning the locations of your stuff to better fit your life.

As a final step, once you've found space for everything in the area you've been decluttering, move all the things that don't go in that room or space to the place that they'll go in according to your Minimalist Mission Statement. If you've already edited that room, find spots for the additional items now. If you haven't, just place the new items in the room and find spots for them once your schedule takes you to that area. Step back. Smile. You've just completed one area of your new minimalist home. Congratulations.

Perseverance

I emphasize creating a fresh, welcoming space before I cover what to do with all the items you've just decluttered for an important reason: this is hard work. Simplifying your life can be exhausting, emotional, and dusty. You've got to see your accomplishments, room-by-room, along the way or you might forget why you're doing this project. The rewards of more life — more joy, better health, and more creativity — can start coming to you right now, as soon as you get started.

In addition to creating your ideal spaces one room at a time, there are a couple other strategies you can employ to make sure you persevere and finish decluttering your home. The first is accountability. The more people you tell about your desires for simplicity, the better. You may want to consider going public on Facebook or Twitter so people can support you. Post something like "Just read *Minimalist Living*, by the brilliant and genius Genevieve Parker Hill and I'm inspired! I'm going to declutter my home and simplify my life by _____ (insert date)." You can, of course, adjust "brilliant and genius" to whichever adjectives you prefer. The point it, the more specific you can be with what you're doing, why you're doing it, and when you're going to be finished, the more effective this technique is. Going public generally makes us more likely to uphold our commitments to ourselves, because we want to be seen as holding true to our word and having integrity. If you're the only one who knows your commitment, it's too easy to let yourself off the hook.

If you'd like to share your intentions with a community of likeminded people (and me!) you can post your decluttering plans to our community of minimalist living enthusiasts on Facebook. Go to **www.facebook.com/mnmlstlvng**

Finally, keep your motivation to persevere in creating fresh new spaces in your home and life strong by proper pacing. Only you can decide what your schedule allows for. Only you can make the time you need to simplify your life. Make sure you allow yourself a generous amount of time so that this project can be fun. For some people, a challenge is motivating. For example, "I will declutter my home by the holidays!" creates a sense of excitement and vision. Others will have more fun with it if they relax and give themselves an easy-to-reach deadline. Try dividing your home up into rooms or smaller areas of your home and setting up a schedule. Just make sure that you do a little bit every day, or you may lose momentum.

Next, let's consider the pile of stuff that is waiting for you to deal with it so that it can bring joy to someone else's life.

CHAPTER EIGHT

What to Do With All That Stuff

"One can furnish a room very luxuriously by taking out furniture rather than putting it in."

– Francis Jourdain

At 3:30 pm on a late summer day in England, Hilary and Bruce began a very special campfire evening. They had taken their boat to one of their favorite remote spots, and with them they had two huge bags of cards they'd given each other through the years. These cards, numbering 500 or so, were the written proof of their thirty-year romance. Over the course of three hours, they read the cards from birthdays, anniversaries, and Valentines Days past, and then set fire to them. They were fulfilling a plan that came about when they both realized that if anything should happen to one of them, it would be too heartbreaking for the one left alone to read them all. Keeping them felt like unnecessary hoarding. During the burning, they shared wine and hundreds of reminders of the love between them. They identified a few of the most special cards to keep in a small treasure box. The rest are now ash.

The experience this couple shared is a wonderful and creative example of the proper use, enjoyment, and disposal of really special belongings. It was a unique experience they created that was tailored to their own romance. It's certainly not for everyone. Their daughter Caroline reported mixed emotions about it. "I can't decide if this is a desperately romantic or desperately sad way to eliminate the tangible evidence of a lifetime of love," she wrote. For some, the idea of a similar campfire would be unappealing. But the important thing is that they made their choice that the bags of cards were becoming a burden, and that their life would be freer without them. They decided to dispose of them in a way that was both reflective and celebratory. Their method and the outcome matched their vision for their lives, and I applaud them for that.

A huge bag of cards from your significant other is an unusual category of stuff. Let's talk about a more normal category of stuff — all the things that you've been editing away as you go about creating fresh new spaces in your home.

Once your transitional box fills up with a day, a week or a month's worth of no-longer-needed items, it's time to sort through it. You can do this as often as you prefer, or only once in a while. Allow a pile to build up, but don't allow it to become so overwhelming that you begin to put off sorting it. If you're using the faster blaze method, your transitional box is likely to fill up much faster, so sort accordingly. In fact, blazers may want to have someone else sort to keep the speed of the process since otherwise the process could easily slip into gazing as you come face to face with what you've gotten rid of.

Whoever is going to do the sorting, create a staging area in your home, garage, or basement that will be available for the purpose of sorting until the end of your paring down project. Divide your staging into seven sections using boxes, bins, or simply piles with signs:

1. Sell
2. Give Away
3. Recycle
4. Special Items
5. Ask Someone Else
6. Clean, Repair, Maintenance
7. Trash

Label the first box, bin, or pile "sell." Put things that have financial value and are easy to sell in this area. At the end of your simplifying project, or when the "sell" pile becomes too big, have a yard sale, trunk sale, or find another way to get a few bucks for your stuff. In the U.S., yards sales typically happen on Saturdays and begin early. Prospective buyers are used to getting up early to get a chance at finding what for them could be a treasure. Put up signs around your neighborhood and consider listing your yard sale on *Craigslist* or one of many new yardsale helper apps for smart phones. For guidance on things that are easy to sell in your area, check *Craigslist* or an app like LetGo in your part of the country. See what people are frequently selling – that's probably also what people are buying. For example, does there seem to be a strong market for couches? Birdcages? Antique tractors? Having the "sell" items all in one area will allow you to sell them all quickly when the time comes.

Here's a hint that I've used for quicker, more profitable sales: tell your story to people. Whether it's that you're selling your stuff to travel the world, you've gotten a divorce and are starting a new life, or simply that you're starting a new adventure in minimalism, people like to know the story behind the stuff. Having a deadline, i.e., "This couch needs to be picked up by Friday," helps speed things as well.

For inspiration on selling to make money to pay off debts, check out the *ManvsDebt* blog. Their motto is, "Sell your crap. Pay off your debt. Do what you love."

In the second area, place items that you don't have the time and energy to sell, that you'd like to give to a friend or charity you think would appreciate them, or that don't have much financial value. As long as the things in this category might have value to someone, you can donate them to a charity. Again, this is more efficiently taken care of in a big batch. There are some fun ways to give things away. When my husband and I were emptying our apartment in preparation for moving abroad, we threw a Valentine's Day party. In the corner, we had a shelf of free stuff and we mentioned to all of our guests that they could take anything they wanted from the shelf. It's a low-pressure way to allow your friends to take what they want but not *have* to. Betsy Warren of the *MarriedWithLuggage* blog had a "reverse birthday party" to give away 39 of her favorite items to friends on her 39th birthday. These are both great ideas to get your friends and family involved in your minimizing process. This is another area where you can use your creativity and come up with fun ideas to make this project enjoyable.

In section three, place items that can be recycled. Check with your local municipal services or use the website *Earth911.com* to find out where and what you can recycle in your area.

Next to recycling, place special items that can't be taken to a standard recycling center. These things include automotive items, electronics, batteries, paint, and pharmaceuticals. Again, use *Earth911.com* to find out where to dispose of these items. Unneeded or expired prescription drugs can usually be taken back to the pharmacy where you obtained them for proper disposal that doesn't put them into the groundwater supply.

The items you need to ask other people about go in area five. Examples of these things are: family heirlooms that don't have a place in your home but that another family member might want, things that belong to someone else, or things that need the help or attention of someone else before they can be used. Storing things for other people – relatives, for example – is fine, as long as it's in the spirit of your Minimalist Mission Statement. My grandmother gave me a writing desk that I cherish, but since I couldn't bring it with me while traveling, it's gracing the guest bedroom of my parent's house right now while I travel the world. It's important to note that just because you have your offspring's stuff in your home doesn't mean you're obligated to hang onto it for them. Don't store other people's things out of guilt or a sense of obligation. Your space is yours to do what you like with. Your children will understand if you explain to them that your home is no longer storage space. Area five can also hold things you're undecided on; talk through your feelings on those items with the appropriate person. Hilary and Bruce's wedding cards from the opening story would be a good example of items to put in this category.

In area six, put things that need your attention for cleaning, repair, or maintenance before they can be used, sold, or given away. Your favorite kitchen knife that needs to be professionally sharpened, the watch that needs a new battery before you give it to your niece, and the blender that needs to be deep-cleaned before you sell it are all examples of things that fit into this category.

In area seven, place a large trash can – preferably one with wheels. This will hold all the trash you'll come across as you go through each room of your home. This is the "end of the line," for things that didn't find a home in one of the previous six sections. Throwing away consumer goods isn't ideal, and a surprising number of things can be recycled or repurposed by someone else or by an organization. Recycling and repurposing are much better than adding to landfills. However, if finding alternative ways to get rid of something is overwhelming or is causing you to procrastinate or become stuck in your decluttering process, don't hesitate to simply throw things away. Start fresh and commit to a less consumer-based lifestyle as your way of honoring the Earth.

Continue the paring down process as outlined in the last two chapters. Edit section by section, room by room, creating fresh new spaces, and then sorting regularly and selling, giving away, recycling, or trashing your stuff when you run out of room in your staging area.

Be patient, pace yourself, and have fun. Hold yourself to the timeline you set, and don't let anyone else guilt, persuade, or browbeat you into going faster – or into slowing down.

How to Let Go of Meaningful Items

Generally the hardest things to let go of are meaningful or sentimental items. You don't have to let all of your meaningful items go, of course. But they are often the most burdensome element among our earthly goods. The feelings they bring up are so complex, that sorting through them can be a source of fear and a reason for procrastination or denial. Even if you keep most of your meaningful items, consider sorting through them and figuring out why they are meaningful for you. I recommend recording these answers in some way, as they are bound to be enlightening. Realizing that the value of each meaningful belonging is almost always in the emotions and stories it provokes, rather than in the thing itself, frees us to let many of these items go.

One way to decide what to keep and what to display for your enjoyment and positive feelings is to create a treasure box and hide it away for a few weeks or months.

Hilary did this while her things where in storage when her new home was being completed. She writes, "I don't normally have a 'box of treasures.' It was only because all our things are now in storage and I didn't want some things to be lost and so I put them aside in a box. There are more special cards and letters from family and friends, a childhood doll, jewelry of my grandmother's and mother's, special presents from Bruce, some photos and special ornaments. Amazingly, only eight weeks on from packing them up I can't remember what half of them are. So I wonder now how much I actually need them."

If you already have a box of meaningful treasures stored somewhere, you can make use of this idea right now. Think about what is in the box. Try to remember; write down a list. Then check the list against the actual contents of the box. You might discover that the things you wrote down are the most important to you, and you can release the rest. Or, you might be surprised that you forgot about something that gives you great happiness. That discovery is an excellent reason to display that item or store it nearby where you can see it or touch it anytime.

I recommend that with each meaningful item, you choose to either record the memory and the "spirit" of the item and release it, or that you display it so it can give you joy all the time. Whether you choose to donate unneeded meaningful items or to keep them, there are three things you can do to make sure your happy-making things are indeed lifting your mood daily or that the essence of them is preserved for future generations: recording, digitizing, and miniaturizing.

Recording, Digitizing, & Miniaturizing

Before letting them go, we must make sure that we capture and record, as part of our legacy, why meaningful items are so important to us. Recording in this context simply means capturing the essence or energy of a thing – the stories, memories, and emotions that a specific meaningful item sparks in you. It could mean taking photos of the belonging, or having a friend or family member record you using a video camera as you talk about the item and tell stories about it. It could mean writing about the item or speaking into a voice recorder about the item. The important thing is that you record what the heirloom or meaningful belonging means to you, and why. It's also vital that what you record can be passed along easily from generation to generation. Think of this as a testimony of what significance this item has provided to you and your family.

Here are some questions to consider as you write the story of your most cherished things:

- How did I come to possess this item?

- How old is it?

- Is there a story related to how it entered my family?

- What does it mean to me?

- What does it remind me of?

- How does this item make me feel, exactly?

- What relationships does it remind me of?

- Where, geographically, are my memories of this item associated?

- Are there songs, sounds, tastes, smells, or other sensations attending my memories of this item?

- What historical events were happening concurrent to the time I acquired this item or remember this item being used?

- What has it taught me?

- Why do I value this item above others like it?

- Does it have financial value as well as emotional value?

- Does it have historical or artistic value?

- If I decide to pass it along, what should I tell the new owner?

- What do I hope others will learn from my relationship with this item?

Consider journaling your answers to these questions, or recording them on video or a voice recorder.

Digitization refers to moving things from analog form to a digital form that can be read or accessed by a computer. Often it means scanning photos, cards, certificates, letters, journal entries, and memorabilia so that the scanned image can be stored on a computer as a digital file. If you've used a digital device, such as a digital video or voice recorder to record your thoughts on your meaningful items, then you've already digitized them. If you've handwritten them, or used a typewriter, then you'll want to take the additional step of scanning them so that you'll have a digital copy.

Digital files take up almost zero physical space. However, you'll need to have a computer, a scanner, and probably a digital voice recorder and camera to digitize yourself. If you'd prefer not to do it yourself, there are companies who will take care of this task for you. One such company is ScanDigital. Others you can check out are DigMyPics and ScanCafe. These companies will often allow you to send a shoebox of photos. They return the photos by mail along with the digital files.

Once you've turned your memories into digital files, it's vital that you ensure they are properly backed up. Computers are susceptible to crashing and viruses, and like physical items, to destructive forces like fires and floods. You can back up your digital files by making copies that you store on an external hard drive and keep in a fire-proof safe. You can also back up files with cloud-based storage on the internet using a web application that can be accessed from anywhere in the world with a special username and password that you set. While not susceptible to computer crashes, floods, or house fires, the cloud isn't perfect. There are, as is always the case with the internet, security concerns. However, if you use a reliable and well-established service, like Dropbox, those risks are minimal. Online web applications like Gmail, Facebook, and many more are clouds since files that you don't delete are stored securely online.

If you're a scrapbooking hobbyist and would like to move your photos to digital form while still enjoying scrapbooking, Google "digital scrapbooking" to see how many people share your interest and are learning and teaching about how to transfer the hobby to an online form. If you want to keep copies of your image files in digital form, but also print some to have on hand, consider using a photo-book designing service. These online services allow you to upload your digital photo files and design a book including the photos and whatever text you'd like to add. They print the book for you, often allowing you to choose from a variety of sizes, and ship it to your doorstep.

Miniaturizing, in the decluttering sense, means taking something and somehow decreasing the amount of space it takes up, usually by keeping only a part of it. An example of miniaturizing is framing a piece of lace from your mother's already torn wedding veil and displaying it next to a photo of her wearing her gown and veil on the special day. You might give away or repurpose the remainder of the lace from the veil, but keeping a small piece of it brings texture and atmosphere when displayed next to the photo of your mother on her wedding day. Another example of miniaturizing is keeping only a symbolic selection of a group or collection of similar things. This might be appropriate if, for example, you've been saving your children's sports trophies. Take a picture of all of them, and then save just one or two of the group. Miniaturizing is often the answer to the question of how to save the spirit of your meaningful items without allowing them to take over your space.

CHAPTER NINE

Maintaining Minimalism

"Simplicity involves unburdening your life, and living more lightly with fewer distractions that interfere with a high quality of life, as defined uniquely by each individual."

– Linda Breen Pierce

Are you inspired? Happy with the changes you've made or dreamed about making to your life and home? That's wonderful! Let's consider how to keep our positive momentum going. To maintain our new, healthier, happier lifestyle, we must choose to do so. We must choose not only to do something differently, i.e., not buying as much stuff and clearing out our old stuff, but to be someone different. In much the same way as dieters are told to begin thinking of themselves as thin even before weight loss occurs, we must begin to think of ourselves as minimalists from now on. Minimalist living must not be only a label; it must become a way of life.

How do you make this lifestyle an ongoing habit? Once you're done paring down, and, in fact, even before you're finished, you must cultivate a new attitude toward your home. If you keep up the old habits of regularly bringing things into your home, all of your hard work will be void and your new minimalist lifestyle mooted. To keep extra things out once you've cleaned and cleared your home will require a paradigm shift -- a change in your beliefs and attitudes.

Let's look at some of the old attitudes and beliefs about home you may have had:

- I'm unaware of or not responsible for my home's atmosphere.

- Stuff just gathers and multiplies like it has a mind of its own.

- I don't really notice how or why my stuff is affecting (or afflicting) me.

- When someone gives me something, I keep it in case they come over and ask about it.

- I'm overwhelmed and stressed when I move around my house.

- I can't find what I need because I have too much clutter.

- I have closets or storage areas that are unusable because they are loaded to the gills.

- My house is just an ordinary place where I live in the spaces around my stuff.

Hopefully, the attitudes above are now shifting to these new attitudes:

- I create and take responsibility for the atmosphere of my home.

- I am in control of all my stuff.

- Everything around me is there for my use, pleasure, or to add meaning to my life.

- When someone gives me something, I keep it if I like it; otherwise I give it away with no guilt.

- I love moving around my home; being clutter free gives me a sense of freedom.

- I easily and quickly find what I need when I'm looking for it.

- I have available storage space for gathering future clutter on its way out the door.

- My home is a sacred place.

Attitude shifts are a result of new habits. Habits are affected by attitudes. Therefore, adjust both your actions and your attitudes. Take to heart the proverb, "As a man thinketh in his heart, so is he." Attitude is what you "thinketh" in your heart, and your actions will reflect those attitudes. To shift your attitude, it helps to adjust your behavior and habits. Behaviors take around 30 days to become ingrained as habits, so don't expect to change yourself overnight. Here are some new habits you can begin working on that will result in your ability to maintain a minimalist lifestyle:

Repeat affirmations daily. Tell yourself "I am in control of my stuff," or other ideas from the "new attitudes" list above.

Study places you consider sacred such as churches, temples, or beautiful spots in nature. See how they are treated and designed, whether by humans or by nature, and apply what you learn to your home.

Post your Minimalist Mission Statement in your home permanently. Perhaps incorporate it into your décor by framing it, cross-stitching it onto a pillow, or stenciling it onto a wall or favorite piece of furniture.

Put things back or clean things up immediately after using them.

Become the gatekeeper of your home, making sure that for every non-consumable item that comes in, one goes out.

Even if you don't have a lot, a home can look cluttered if everything isn't in its place. Yet, sometimes, life prevents us from putting everything away immediately after we use it. More often, the people we live with may not share our desire to have "everything in its place, and a place for everything." For these days, and people, enter the pickup basket. Your pickup basket is where things gather during moments in the day when you don't have time to put them back. It keeps the clutter off surfaces and stores it for you until you have time to put it away. When you do have time, it makes it easier on you because you can pick up the basket and walk it around the house, depositing things in their rightful places.

Maintaining minimalism should be fun. If you don't get some satisfaction or enjoyment out of it, you won't keep it up. Find a way to make it fun for you, whether that means playing music, turning it into a game, or getting others to help you.

Life Events

Big life events and transitions are the biggest obstacle to keeping your minimalist habits. Moving to a new place, moving in with a partner or getting married, and having a baby are all massive transitions with their own challenges to maintaining minimalism.

Moving to a larger home adds temptation to the list of challenges. With all that extra space, it may be all you can do not to purchase things simply to fill it. If you have the space, it's much easier to bring things home. Yet if the outcome of having a larger home is filling it with stuff you don't use or need, then your new home will just add stress to your life, which is probably not the reason you chose to move into a larger home in the first place. To fight the urge to fill empty space, consider why you decided to move into a larger home. Was it to have more room for children, or visitors? In that case, set up the extra space to reflect its intended purpose. If you have a guest bedroom, make if comfortable for guests with new sheets, soft towels, and anything else your guests need to have an enjoyable stay with you.

Moving in with a partner or getting married is a huge life transition that brings with it a chance to double your belongings, if not triple them. When two people live together, they must agree, or at least tolerate, the others' attitude toward stuff. This can be difficult, as attitudes toward our surroundings vary widely. Using the strategies from Chapter Five, you may be able to decide whether the two of you will be minimalists together, or whether you need to pursue minimalist living on your own.

Adding a new bundle of joy to your family is another special case where your normally minimalist lifestyle can suddenly turn into a festival of stuff collection. "Mommy guilt," or "Daddy guilt," can come into play when your quest to be the best parent you can be is taken advantage of my marketers and well-meaning friends. The former may tap into your desire to keep your baby happy and safe by telling you that their product will fit the bill. The latter may innocently suggest this or that product as a way to improve your baby's life. If you're new to parenthood, you may doubt your own abilities and think you need to take action on stuff-related advice. Fortunately, this is not the case. Lynn from a comment on an article called "31 and Pregnant: Minimalist Mom vs. Baby Stuff," on

Chambanamoms.com, comments, "My daughter is almost 8 months old. Don't let the hyperbole get to you. These things are actually absolutely necessary: a place for the baby to sleep, diapers and wipes, things to keep the baby warm, a place to bathe the baby, a car seat, and food for the baby. That's it. Everything else is a nice-to-have." [15]

Holidays and Celebrations

On occasions when gift exchanges are expected, how do we maintain minimalism? One way is by focusing on our inner lives and our relationships during the holidays and during other celebrations, like birthdays. Focusing on what's important during the holidays seems to be getting increasingly difficult. Recently a friend of mine posted her thoughts on Facebook after getting ads from companies that were open on Thanksgiving Day:

Rarely do I ever post frustrations on Facebook but I am so mad after checking my email this morning and seeing

---

[15]   Lynn commenting on Jennifer S. Wilson, "31 and Pregnant: Minimalist Mom vs. Baby Stuff," May 3, 2011,
http://www.chambanamoms.com/2011/05/03/31-and-pregnant-minimalist-mom-vs-baby-stuff/.

promotional emails from several stores that I frequent saying they are open ON thanksgiving... As if midnight isn't bad enough!!!!!!

I unsubscribed from their email lists and left an emotionally charged comment. Although I am only one person I let them know I would never step foot in their stores again!!! I encourage all of you to do the same!!!!

This is the problem with our society the obsession with things and not relationships is tearing families and our world apart! Please look at the places you frequent most! If they are open today don't go back and send a message to these money hungry CEOs!

Sorry Happy Thanksgiving everyone! I hope everyone gets time with family AT HOME.

We can each make a difference if we make it clear that shopping is not what the holidays are about.

Now that your home is decluttered, save yourself the time and energy of having to do that again by keeping it this way. Once the editing and disposal process is finished, you'll only be maintaining what you've done, which takes a lot less energy than the original process. In the next part of this book, we'll talk more about why minimalism is so important to a fulfilled, purposeful life.

CHAPTER TEN

Minimalism and Your Purpose

When we're old and gray, we won't wax poetic on the things we had—but rather on what we did in the spaces between them."

– Francine Jay

So what are you going to do with your life now that you've emptied it of burdensome clutter and created new space, both in your home and in your schedule? Perhaps you already know exactly what you're going to do with your newfound space. Or maybe you don't, and you're having some unexpected feelings of fear. The empty space can be downright terrifying, like a black hole, or an endless void. Acknowledge the fear; admit it. Fear is often a signpost that you should run far away from a hungry predator or threatening enemy (or punch it in the face). It can also signal that you're doing something powerful, new, and positive in your life. The animal brain that makes up part of each human brain likes the safety and comfort of the known. When we are in uncharted territory, that part of our brain can kick in and tell us to hurry back to comfortsville. But in this case, we just listen to what our brain is telling us, and then respond "Thanks, but I'm going to stay here and get used to this new territory."

Sometimes, we will feel terrified because we've been avoiding the bigger questions in life, such as "What am I going to do with the rest of my life?" Clutter can be a distraction from your true purpose. Once the extra stuff is out of your life, the fear may be telling you to quickly get some clutter back in your home, your schedule, or your brain so that you can avoid facing the big questions.

Instead of recluttering, fill the void with what you're truly meant to do in your life. How are you going to let your fresh new attitude and creativity add zest to your days? Your answer will depend on your purpose, the deep inner understanding of why you're here that only you can discover. Perhaps you've already discovered your purpose; if so, minimalist living can help you live out your purpose more fully now that you have the time and space to do so.

Eckhart Tolle writes that if we identify with our things, then it's going to be difficult – likely impossible – to remove them from our lives. For example, most of us identify with our bodies. We, in some sense, are our bodies. No one willingly relinquishes an arm or a leg. Identifying with our possessions isn't that much different. In a way, it's insane to identify with our things. We are not our stuff. Yet in our culture, it's remarkably easy to begin to associate our belongings with our identity. We need to stop allowing things to define us, and instead, allow our purpose to define who we are.

If you aren't sure of your purpose, aren't certain of the reason why you're here and how you will contribute to your community and the world, then minimalist living can help you uncover it. Once you've simplified your life, you're free to use the tools that can help you discover your purpose. These tools are what Martha Beck calls "spiritual technologies." These are proven methods to help you connect with the universe, God, your subconscious mind, inner knowing, or whatever you call that which connects us all. Some of these tools include meditation, following your heart, prayer, self-care, and practicing gratitude and mindfulness. Each of us must follow a unique path to find our purpose. Purpose is irremovably entwined with spirituality. You may find your purpose through the spiritual tools that appeal to you in combination with external factors such as life opportunities that arise, people who come into your life, and simply the power of serendipity. Being open to finding your purpose by setting an intention to do so and then living your life receptive to your heart's deepest desires is a great way to start. Pursue a spiritual path to connect to your purpose.

When I say "spiritual," know that I'm referring to matters of the heart and soul. I'm talking about anything in life that makes you feel whole, fulfilled, and connected to your fellow human beings and to the universe. For one person, a spiritual experience could be camping by a pristine mountain lake. For another, it could be worshipping with others in a church. I'm not necessarily referring to anything religious unless that is where you find your connection with your own soul and those of others.

To 'own' something -- what does it really mean? What does it mean to make something 'mine'? [...] Many people don't realize until they are on their deathbed and everything external falls away that nothing ever had anything to do with who they are. In the proximity of death, the whole concept of ownership stands revealed as ultimately meaningless.

[...] 'Blessed are the poor in spirit,' Jesus said, 'for theirs will be the kingdom of heaven.' What does 'poor in spirit' mean? No inner baggage, no identifications. Not with things, nor with any mental concepts that have a sense of self in them. And what is the 'kingdom of heaven'? The simple but profound joy of Being that is there when you let go of identifications and so become 'poor in spirit.' – Eckhart Tolle, *A New Earth.*

Tolle emphasizes presence ("Being") and also a disassociation of our identity from our belongings. We are taught to find our joy in being, not in what we own. We are not (necessarily) going to go so far as to say the best way to live is to give away *all* our stuff. The best way for you to live is in the way that you choose.

Your life will be enriched when you start acting from a deep inner purpose informed by your spirituality. We're focusing: we're thinking more about our belongings and we're taking action so that what we have is helping us, not hurting us spiritually. When we bring our attention to anything, our level of awareness and consciousness increases and this allows us to make better choices about that thing. For example, you've often heard the advice that if you're trying to watch your diet, you should write down what you're eating. In a similar way, when we are focusing on our true purpose, we are less likely to consume mindlessly.

This can become a spiritual practice. If we allow it to, it can make us feel more grateful about our life. For example, if instead of watching a TV commercial and desiring the product that we see, we instead look around our home and see the things that bring us so much joy, that are so useful to our lives, and that help us live our purpose. We now have a positive emotion of gratitude instead of a false, artificially created desire for something that we don't need and that will only clutter up our house. The physical lightness that comes from editing our collection of stuff becomes a spiritual lightness. Think about the lightheartedness you have when you begin a journey. You leave your home with only a bag or two. You feel a sense of optimism because in a way, you're as free as you'll ever be. You can have that feeling of freedom all the time if you cultivate gratitude for what you do have and a minimalist's approach to acquisition.

Here's the heart of the message of this book: it's not any one thing that has precious value; it's your intangible connection to the thing that is precious. Your unique set of memories, values, and lessons learned through your experiences, relationships, and yes, through your stuff, over the course of your life are what's important.

Use these experiences and the way you have grown around them to make the world a better place.

Making Room for Better

There's a phenomenon I've noticed that is so common I casually call it the "law of making space." I've noticed that if you have space for more, you'll acquire stuff to fill that space. I mentioned this when I talked about how moving into a bigger house often means attracting things to fill all that extra room. Thrillingly, this seems to be a law we can apply to the spiritual world as well. If you create space, many more opportunities to fill that space will come to you then would if you had never made the space. Your job is to stay connected to your spirit so that you can recognize what will fill the space for your highest good. When we get in touch with our deepest heart's desires through a spiritual practice, we know what we want. We can take action to be, do, and have what we desire, spiritually speaking. For example, if you desire to feel deeply connected to friends who nurture, support, and love you, first make space. This may mean spending less time with people who denigrate, criticize, or make you feel bad. There will always be a small space of loneliness or emptiness before the space is filled with something better. By taking a step in faith to make room, the higher quality you seek will come to you because there is room in your life. I had an acquaintance who was single for a long time and very much wanted to be married. But her refrain was, "At least I'm not with the wrong person. It's better to be alone than in an unhealthy relationship." She knew about the law of making space. She kept the "boyfriend spot," open in her life for as long as it took. Now she's been happily married to Mr. Right for over a year.

I recently talked to a friend who was having trouble getting rid of some clothes. She no longer wore them, but they represented a time in her life when she felt independent, affluent, and attractive. She wanted to make space in her life, but was afraid to lose the reminder of the powerful memories and emotions those clothes held. I helped her come up with other ways to remember the good times she had wearing those clothes, ways that will allow her to release the clothes to improve someone else's life and make space in her closet. Once she clears her closet, there will be a season of emptiness. This is a natural lull before something better comes to her. Eventually new clothes – even better clothes – will come into her life. Yet even more exciting on a spiritual and energetic level is that she now has room for a new spiritual season of her life to begin. She'll be clothed in even more joy. By letting go of the good, she'll experience the great.

Appeal to your intuition and spirit about areas of your life in which decluttering may have spiritual benefits. I hope this is a fruitful area for you to realize a deeper connection to joy and light.

A Fresh Start

Minimalist living is really just a starting point for authentic living. We need open spaces – blank canvases – upon which we can occupy ourselves more deeply with the art of living. Minimalism is intentional life design. By removing distractions, obstacles, and buildup, we live life as we truly desire, with the values that we select, not those selected for us by convention, copywriters or trend setters. Today my hope is that this book has helped and inspired you to create more open space to play in – space that invigorates your health, sets you on a path of purpose and sparks inner healing and joy for you.

Resources on Minimalist Living

I invite you to sign up for the free 3-Day Decluttering Challenge at SimpleLivingToolkit.com so that I can send you a short and sweet email series to help you jump start and maintain your simplified lifestyle.

Here are some additional resources I have found valuable on my own minimalism journey.

Further Reading on Minimalism, Decluttering, and Simple Living

Clutter Rehab: 101 Tips and Tricks to Become an Organization Junkie and Love It! By Laura Wittmann

Simplify by Joshua Becker

Unstuff Your Life! By Andrew J. Mellen

You Can Buy Happiness (and It's Cheap): How One Woman Radically Simplified Her Life and How You Can Too by Tammy Strobel

Recommended Blogs, Projects and Websites

SimpleLivingToolkit.com – Sign up for the 3-Day Decluttering Challenge and download other free resources. This is an ever-changing resource since I update it regularly with tools to help you live a simple, joyful life.

Facebook.com/mnmlstlvng – "Like" the Minimalist Living Facebook page to join a community of like-minded people pursuing a simpler life. I share great resources and inspiration on minimalist living here.

Zenhabits.net – Leo Babauta writes about finding simplicity in the daily chaos of our lives. It's about clearing the clutter so we can focus on what's important, create something amazing, and find happiness. He also has another blog that's even more minimalist at mnmlist.com.

TheMinimalists.com – Joshua Fields Millburn & Ryan Nicodemus write about living a meaningful life with less stuff for their audience of more than 100,000 monthly readers. They have been featured in the Wall Street Journal, CBS, USA Today, NBC, and many more outlets.

MissMinimalist.com – Author Francine Jay writes, "by writing about minimalism, I hope to promote it as a lifestyle alternative. I want others who are dissatisfied with consumer culture to know they're not alone. I think it would be wonderful — for ourselves, for the

Earth, and its other inhabitants—if we all learned to live with a little bit less."

ZeroWasteHome.blogspot.com – Bea Johnson writes about the happier, more fulfilling lifestyle she and her family began enjoying when they downsized their home and began living a zero waste lifestyle. She provides helpful tips on the blog on how to "refuse, reduce, reuse, recycle, rot (and only in that order)."

TheMinimalistMom.com – Rachel Jonat writes about her family's journey to living with only what they need, and how her family paid off $60,000 in debt in one year, partly through embracing a minimalist lifestyle.

BeMoreWithLess.com – Courtney Carver writes about simplifying to live a life with more joy and less stress. Her site's archive is extensive and free.

Made in the USA
Coppell, TX
25 April 2021

54519914R00079